Fun & Easy
INTARSIA PROJECTS

Acknowledgments

The authors extend their most sincere thanks and appreciation to our typist Jennifer Blahnik and our graphic artist Roxanne LeMoine. We also wish to acknowledge our spouses Anna Droege and Patricia Spielman for their unwavering support and generous assistance with this work.

Library of Congress Cataloging-in-Publication Data

Spielman, Patrick E.
   Fun & easy intarsia projects/ Patrick Spielman and Frank Droege.
      p. cm.
   Includes index.
   ISBN 1-4027-1623-0
   1. Marquetry. I. Title: Fun and easy intarsia project. II. Droege, Frank. III. Title.

TT192.S65 2005
745.51'2--dc22

                                    2005001144

2 4 6 8 10 9 7 5 3 1

Published by Sterling Publishing Co., Inc.
387 Park Avenue South, New York, NY 10016
© 2005 by Patricia Spielman and Frank Droege.
Distributed in Canada by Sterling Publishing
c/o Canadian Manda Group, 165 Dufferin Street
Toronto, Ontario, Canada M6K 3H6
Distributed in Great Britain by Chrysalis Books Group PLC
The Chrysalis Building, Bramley Road, London W10 6SP, England
Distributed in Australia by Capricorn Link (Australia) Pty. Ltd.
P.O. Box 704, Windsor, NSW 2756, Australia

Sterling ISBN 1-4027-1623-0

For information about custom editions, special sales, premium and corporate purchases, please contact Sterling Special Sales Department at 800-805-5489 or specialsales@sterlingpub.com

Contents

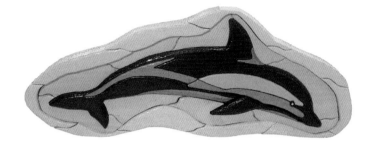

Introduction

All of the designs in this book can be made using inexpensive wood materials, basic tools, and fundamental techniques. The resulting projects are colorful works of wood art that are probably best described as "painted intarsia" (**I–1**).

Some of the projects, however, may be stained and/or naturally finished (**I–2**). There are some other projects that incorporate a combination of processes, but almost all will more or less come under the broad and contemporary classification of intarsia. Some woodworkers may also call this work "wood mosaic," "dimensional inlay," or "segmentation," which we did in our earlier book *Creative Scroll Saw Segmentation*.

The term "intarsia" originally defined an early Italian process of inlaying various colored woods into a wood background. Today, however, intarsia work involves very little, if any, actual inlay work (**I–3**).

Current intarsia publications by and large focus on technique instructions for three-dimensional shaping and the fitting of various kinds and colors of natural solid-wood pieces together at their edges. Once cut, shaped and smoothed, the pieces are glued onto (not into) a flat surface, which is usually a piece of thin plywood called a backer (**I–4**).

I–1. **This colorful painted intarsia was made from a single piece of material. All edges of each piece were rounded slightly, individually painted, and glued to a plywood backer.**

Typically, contemporary intarsia work also requires the use of multiple species and colors of wood. Frequently, special kinds of wood are specified to achieve uncommon colors. They often include exotic, rare, or expensive woods that may be difficult to obtain.

I–2. Stained dimensional intarsia. Here the background pieces were reduced in thickness to elevate the design elements at multiple levels of relief.

I–3. Painted intarsia piece actually inlaid into the surface of a purchased wooden plate.

I–4. These examples of contemporary intarsia by noted author and designer Lucille Crabtree feature a variety of woods in their natural colors.

Conversely, every project in this book is made from readily available softwoods and plywoods that are easy and safe to work with. The painted intarsia projects included here are fun, fast to cut, inexpensive, and much more colorful than intarsia work that relies upon a selection of natural wood to achieve color variety.

In painted intarsia, the project design is cut out utilizing the speed and very fine kerf- and detail-cutting capability afforded by the modern scroll saw (I–5). There is virtually no wood waste because most pieces are cut from one single piece of material.

The edges of the individual pieces are rounded over or otherwise contoured and sanded. Each piece is individually painted or stained, and glued onto a flat plywood backer to complete the total design.

This book provides 50 designs with ready-to-use patterns that may be enlarged to any size desired using an office copy machine. Most are flat-backed projects that can be hung on a wall. We also provide a dozen or more examples of these designs incorporated into functional

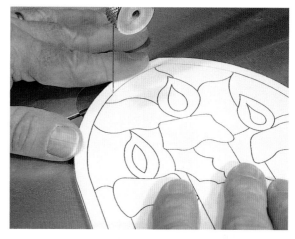

I–5. Components of a painted intarsia project being cut. Just one pattern and one piece of material is required.

projects, including cabinet doors, tabletops, clocks, and the boxes shown in I–6.

All patterns and projects are designed for woodworkers at all stages from entry level to advanced. There are many design subjects to choose from: rural or country, floral, folk art, humorous, abstract, Native American, animals, Christmas, classic, and even an inspirational quotation in cut-out signage.

I–6. Boxes with intarsia lids are just two of many functional art projects that can be made by interchanging the variety of design choices and patterns given in this book.

CHAPTER 1

Wood Materials, Supplies, and Tools

There are very few essential or special items necessary to get started. Some wood, access to an office copy machine, a drill, a scroll saw, and some basic gluing and finishing supplies will get you going. As with any craft, there are always some optional accessories that make one's efforts easier, faster, and just more fun. This chapter provides brief discussions of the essentials and also describes some of the optional accessories.

Wood Materials

Solid Woods

No. 2 shop pine, northern white cedar, western red cedar, and basswood are very suitable woods and generally easy to obtain (1–1). Other domestic softwoods prevalent in your locality should be considered. If necessary, standard ¾-inch stock can be resawn to make thinner material for smaller projects. Three-quarter-inch material can be glued face to face to make thicker chunks such as stock for scroll- or band-sawn boxes. The basic requirements are that the wood be dry and have some areas without

1–1. Pine, red cedar, white cedar, and basswood are good, inexpensive choices for solid woods.

typical defects such as knots and checks. Material stains and small defects that can be covered by paint are usually acceptable.

Plywood

Just about any kind of plywood ⅛ to ¼ inch thick is suitable for backer material (1–2). Recycled wall paneling is an especially good choice for backing material since it is typically not visible and it usually has one good gluing surface.

Only tight-core, imported metric plywoods such as Baltic or Finnish birch and poplar

1–2. Plywood. Shown on top of ⅛- and ¼-inch sheets of Baltic birch plywood are two pieces of recycled wall paneling: the finished face on the right and the gluable surface on the left.

Tools and Supplies

Copy Machine

The use of a photocopier is essential for enlarging many of the project patterns. Most public libraries, printing companies, and business communities with a "copy shop" or office supply store have inexpensive copying services. The better copy machines make enlargements or reductions in one percent increments. Remember that the enlargement sizes given on the pattern pages are merely suggestions. Sometimes a slightly smaller enlargement will allow you to use stock that otherwise may be too small. And, conversely, a slightly larger setting will permit the full use of stock that otherwise would be trimmed, with the cutoffs becoming scrap.

Pattern Adhesive

The recommended process is to apply a paper photocopy of the cutting pattern directly to the

should be used for the facing layers that are visible and will be sawn into segments. These materials are available in small quantities by mail order from scroll-sawing supply companies or in full or partial panels from specialty lumber companies and building products centers. One-eight inch (3-mm) 3-ply or ¼-inch (6-mm) 5-ply stock Italian poplar is generally the best value cost-wise, but it may be more difficult to find. Baltic or Finnish birch generally finishes nicely. Ask for a "BB" grade, which is a special grade of material that is designed to be cut up.

Solid-core domestic 3-ply hardwood plywoods are generally intended for architectural uses and often chip out on the face edges or delaminate when cut into small parts with the scroll saw. Their face veneers are usually poorly glued. This kind of plywood, even in the top grades, is best avoided for this type of work.

1–3. A temporary bond spray adhesive mounts a photocopied pattern directly to the workpiece for sawing. Note that the three straight edges were precut.

1–4. This mid-priced 20-inch scroll saw features up-front controls, easy blade changes, variable speed, and a large worktable.

1–5. An economy-model 16-inch bench-top scroll saw with features suitable for making the projects in this book. Notice the auxiliary piece of thin hardboard held in place with double-faced tape. This provides almost zero clearance around the blade, which is necessary for sawing very small parts.

surface of your wood with a temporary bonding spray adhesive (**1–3**). The saw cuts are then made through the pattern and the wood. A light coat of a good adhesive sprayed only on the back of the pattern should allow it to be removed easily when sawing is completed. If too much adhesive or a cheap, poor-quality or the wrong kind of adhesive is used, it will be necessary to soften the adhesive using a rag and some solvent to remove the pattern.

Drilling Tools

A drill press ensures that the small blade-threading holes needed to cut out inside openings will be made perfectly vertical. A good eye and a hand drill with a square guide will also work. Several small fractional or numbered drill bits will get the job done. Those with diameters of ¹⁄₁₆ and ¹⁄₃₂ inch are suitable for most sawing jobs. Very fine drill bits with wire gauge numbers 70 to 80 are available to drill holes smaller than ¹⁄₃₂ inch. The larger the number, the smaller the drill bit.

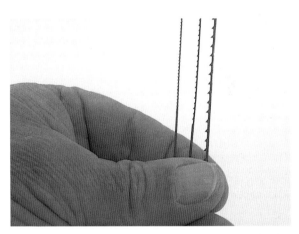

1–6. Basic blades. Left to right: No. 2 and No. 5 blades will handle most jobs; the special thick-wood blade is useful for resawing small pieces to a reduced thickness, but is not essential.

Scroll Saws

Almost any scroll saw capable of carrying plain-end blades can be used with success (**1–4** and **1–5**). Saws with a large throat or a thickness-cutting capacity greater than ¾ inch are not required. Saws with a variable-speed control feature and a quick blade-change capability, however, are preferred over single-speed saws. A slower blade-speed option offers better control when sawing thin, soft material. Higher-end saws are generally more "user-friendly," and provide less blade breakage, less vibration, thicker and larger stock-cutting capacities, plus a variety of other conveniences. Refer to *The New Scroll Saw Handbook* for complete descriptions and specification of scroll saws available today.

Scroll-Saw Blades

Plain-end blades are definitely recommended over the pin-end types. Skip-tooth, double-tooth, and ground skip-tooth blades are all suitable. The ground blades are not available in sizes smaller than No. 5, which is sometimes too large for many of the projects. Larger-sized blades and the special thick wood blades are best for resawing segments and cutting heavy material (1–6). Refer to *The New Scroll Saw*

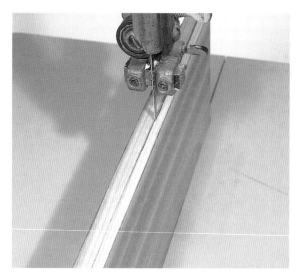

1–7. A bandsaw permits do-it-yourself resawing of solid boards into thin ones, as shown. Plywoods or MDF (medium-density fiberboard) panels of various thicknesses can be obtained for making painted projects.

Handbook for a complete discussion of blades, cutting speeds, and useful tips.

Band Saws

A band saw, like a dust-collecting system, is nice to have but not necessary. As discussed in Chapter 2, a band saw is useful for resawing thicker boards into thinner ones that may be used to make many of the projects in this book (1–7). Solid woods ⅛ and ¼ inch thick and prepared especially for scroll-sawing are now available from many mail-order houses. This material and imported metric plywoods are usable and available. They're just more expensive. Refer to Chapter 2, which describes two resawing processes with a band saw.

Edge-Forming and Shaping Tools

Once the pattern pieces are cut out, the sharp sawn edges need to be rounded over or softened. The amount of round-over or material removal ranges from very little, such as just a ¹⁄₁₆-inch radius on ¼-inch-thick material, to a full ⅜-inch radius on ¾-inch-thick material. Any number of items can be used, including folded sandpaper or even fingernail files for minimal work, to knives, rasps, and files for greater material removal (1–8).

A high-speed rotary tool (1–8) will make this work much faster. Various-sized small sanding drums and inexpensive diamond-coated microburrs (1–9 and 1–10) are available that make the rounding over, chamfering, or shaping of all sizes of work very fast and easy.

Abrasives and Sanding Tools

Larger, flat surfaces can be smoothed by employing typical hand-sanding techniques or with power sanders of choice (1–11 and 1–12).

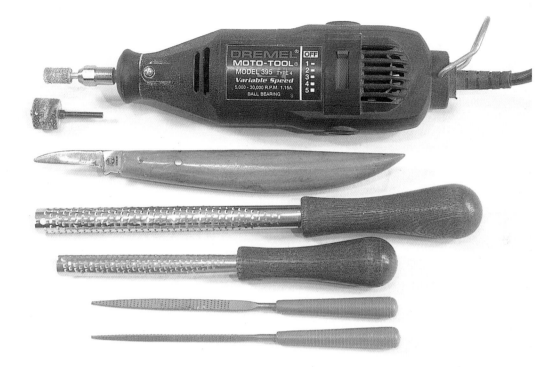

1–8. Tools for rounding over edges, shaping contours, and detailing. Shown from top to bottom: a high-speed rotary tool that carries various small cutters and sanding drums; a knife; small rasps; and files.

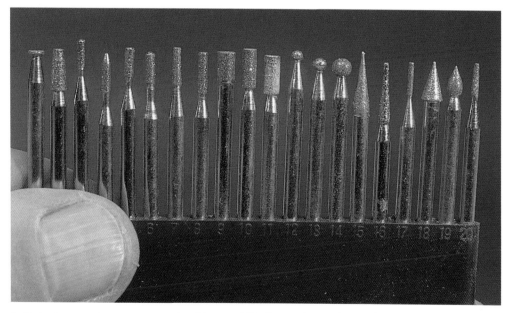

1–9. An inexpensive yet very serviceable set of 20 diamond-coated microburrs on ⅛-inch shanks that cost less than 70 cents each.

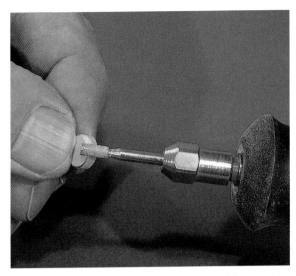

1–10. A close-up showing a rotary diamond burr used to round over the edge of a very small cutout.

1–11. A small pad sander is used to smooth a flat board supported on a nonslip pad.

Paints and Finishing Supplies

Water-based paints, such as acrylic art paints, are recommended because of their good shelf life, abundant color choices, good coverage, and easy clean-up (1–13). Gel-type stains and slightly thinned acrylic paints allow grain patterns to show through if and when the opportunity presents itself. Typical felt-tip markers are fast and convenient for applying color to small parts. Special felt-tip stain markers are also now available (1–14).

Some woods, such as basswood, usually have little grain definition. Having some wood filler or water putty on hand is often useful for filling scroll-saw blade-entry holes, dents, chips, etc. Some cheap sponges and foam and bristle brushes are typical application tools that are also good to have on hand. Aerosol satin acrylic finishes or brush-on flat polyurethane finishes are recommended for a final, post-assembly coating.

1–12. A random orbit sander prepares the surface before mounting the photocopied cutting pattern.

Safety Accessories

Obviously prudent safety procedures should always be observed in every workshop. Personal protection items, including safety goggles,

1–13. Acrylic craft paints, brushes, and a paint pencil designed for adding fine detail lines.

1–14. Consider using felt-tip color and wood stain markers for finishing small pieces.

hearing protectors, and some sort of dust-filtering system are strongly recommended. Other special safety devices to consider include work-holding clamps, push sticks, proper lighting, a shop apron, and, if necessary, proper respirators for protection from any materials that may emit fumes, as well as other hazardous dust or waste. Proper handling, storage, and disposal of flammable materials are other important precautions.

Basic Techniques

In almost every craft, there is usually more than one way to accomplish a given task. This is also true when making the projects in this book. Tooling capabilities and materials available vary from workshop to workshop and each craftsperson must work within his or her own limitations. Individual experimentation is encouraged to personalize and streamline the procedures described in this chapter.

Working in a fully equipped shop affords the luxury of performing more and different procedures than working in one with just the bare essentials of a scroll saw and hand drill. This is especially true when preparing solid-wood materials for a project. If a table saw, joiner, planer, and band saw are not available to prepare the wood, then purchasing stock of the correct size and thickness becomes the primary option. Plywood of suitable thickness is a good option for almost all painted projects (2–1). Use solid wood when making projects with shaped parts or with relief segments that will be stained or naturally finished (2–2). A quality plywood, however, is always a good choice for small or large flat-faced projects (see Chapter 3) because it stays dimensionally stable and does not warp.

2–1. A typical flat-faced project. Depending upon its size, the face pieces are usually cut from ¼-inch-thick solid wood or Baltic birch plywood with a cheaper plywood backing.

Preparing the Patterns

By and large, most patterns in this book are best enlarged to the size of your choice (2–3). This is easily done with an office copy machine. A proportional scale (2–4) is a very helpful accessory for determining enlargement (or reduction) percentages. A proportional scale consists of two discs with scaled divisions that rotate around a common pivot. Once the existing and desired sizes are aligned, the percentage of enlargement or reduction is given in a "window." This allows you to set the copy machine quickly to deliver the desired pattern size without guesswork. Simply align a pattern dimension desired on the outer disc. Then read the percentage in the window.

As a rule, it is a good idea to make at least two identical photocopies of each pattern. One will be used for cutting. The second pattern is for keeping track of pieces by placing them on the pattern as they are cut. The second pattern is sometimes helpful during painting and assembly.

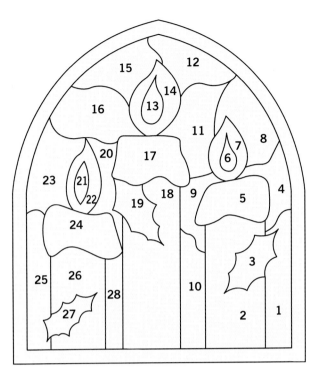

2–3. A typical pattern with each part numbered.

2–2. This multilevel intarsia project is best made from 1-inch solid wood with a ¼-inch plywood backer.

When projects involve many pieces, it is a good idea to number each piece of the project on the pattern prior to cutting, as shown in **2–3**. When necessary, it is also helpful to mark pieces with identifying marks, such as R or L for right and left pieces and to indicate up or down placement.

Preparing Wood Materials

The projects in this book are made from solid wood and/or plywood materials ranging from ⅛ to ¾ inch in thickness. If plywood is used, it only needs to be selected for thickness and quality and then sawn to appropriate width and length. When preparing solid-wood boards, they need to be machined to thickness and sometimes several pieces must be glued edge-to-edge to make a necessary width.

2–4. A proportional scale gives the setting for a photocopier to make a pattern copy at a predetermined size.

2–5. Resawing to thickness following a marked edge.

Resawing

Resawing (2–5 and 2–6) is the process of sawing solid wood to thickness. Resawing techniques may be necessary to make up project panels that will be subsequently scroll-sawn into the project's segments or parts. Resawing techniques may also be applied to reduce the thickness of selected pieces to create relief on the project's face surfaces. This class of resawing work is discussed later.

There are various ways to resaw boards on the band saw. Two not so common, but effective, techniques follow:

Technique No. 1 simply involves following a straight line marked on the edge of a board. To keep the board vertical and prevent it from tipping during cutting, a clamp or drill-press vise provides steady support (2–7 and 2–8).

Technique No. 2 is a more involved process using a shop-made fence (2–9 and 2–10). The advantage of this technique is that once the fence is set up, duplicate thicknesses can be sawn quickly and without marking a cutting line or using the shifting clamps and/or vises.

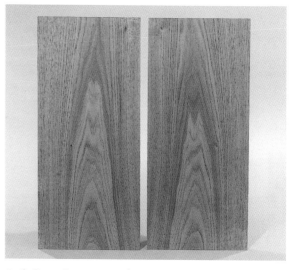

2–6. Resawing may produce two or more usable pieces from one board.

General construction details for making a typical fence and an auxiliary table for a 14-inch band saw are given in 2–11.

Most band saws tend to cut with some "lead" toward one side, so a slight angular feed direction is necessary to compensate. To determine the amount of lead and how to set the fence to correct for lead, proceed as follows:

1. Select a scrap board with a straight edge

2–7. Resawing technique No. 1: A line is followed freehand with the work supported at the start of the cut with a small vise as shown.

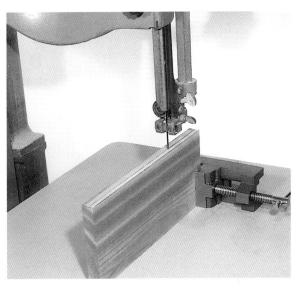

2–8. The vise is moved to the uncut end to complete the cut. The results are surprisingly accurate.

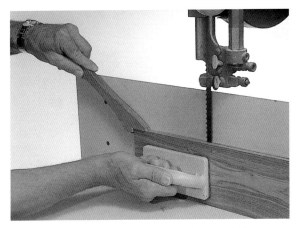

2–9. Resawing technique No. 2: A shop-made fence is clamped to the saw table usually at a slight angle so it compensates for blade "lead." The workpiece is supported against the fence as it is fed into the blade.

2–10. Chunks of dry, dead wood may be economically sawn into boards.

and draw a cutting line about one to two inches parallel to that edge.

2. With a freehand feed, saw along this line. To follow a line, you will soon be compensating your feed direction to correct for "lead." With the blade still in the cut, stop the feed and shut down the saw while holding the board down against the table at the feeding angle. Now, draw a pencil line onto the table following the straight edge of the board.

3. Set and clamp your fence at the resawing thickness (distance from the blade) and with the fence also in a position that is parallel to the line drawn on the table.

4. Make successive resawing cuts as necessary. Keep the stock against the fence with some side pressure (**2–9** and **2–10**).

Smoothing Band-Sawn Surfaces

Surfaces cut with the band saw can be smoothed with a planer, a drum-sanding machine, a portable electric sander (**2–12**) or, if need be, by hand. Workpiece surfaces should be sanded smooth before applying cutting patterns.

Edge-to-Edge Gluing

Depending upon the panel size required and the resawing capacity of the band saw, edge gluing may be done (if necessary) either before or after resawing (**2–13**). In either case, the gluing edges should be machined straight and true with a jointer or a hand plane.

Project Techniques

Adhering Patterns

Enlarge the pattern as desired, and ensure that it will cover the stock (panel size) on hand. Trim the pattern to size with scissors. Apply a light

Band-Saw Ripping and Resawing Fence

7¹⁄₂" x 2 x 10"

¹⁄₈" x 7 x 10"

2¹⁄₂"

¹⁄₈"

4³⁄₄"

2–11. Details for making an auxiliary band-saw table and a high resawing fence.

coat of temporary bonding spray adhesive to the back of the pattern and press it to the best surface of your stock (see **1–3** on *page 10*).

Drilling Blade-Threading Holes

Drilling blade-threading holes is a necessary step when making inside cutouts. Holes can be

2–12. Smoothing a resawn surface.

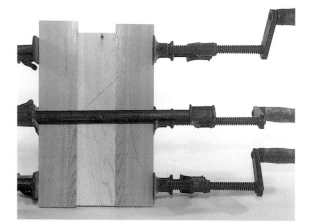

2–13. Boards glued edge-to-edge to make a wide panel.

drilled either directly on the line or just to either side of it (**2–14**). Drilling to one side of the line offers the advantage that if you want to later fill the hole, or the remaining part of it, you need to work on only one piece or segment. Generally, however, when holes are drilled directly on the line, the kerf will consume most of the hole and any small indents remaining will likely be filled with paint or be visually insignificant.

Making Parallel Straight and Curved Cuts

Guide the edge of the workpiece against two fingertips held stationary against the table as shown in **2–15** while the stock is advanced with the other hand. This technique often works well for making true straight-line and smoothly curved border cuts.

Sawing Small Pieces with an Auxiliary Zero-Clearance Table

Sawing very small pieces is a frequent task, and it is easily accomplished when the work is supported all around the blade. Drill a small hole for the blade in some thin sheet material such as plastic, hardboard, or plywood. Then secure it to the scroll-saw table with masking tape or with double-faced tape (**2–16**). This setup prevents small cut pieces from falling through the table opening.

Cutting very small pieces is easy, but you do not want to lose any. This requires that you keep track of the pieces, being certain they do not inadvertently get lost. Keep your work area clean of sawdust and offcuts, and place each cut piece onto an extra copy of the pattern so all pieces can be accounted for throughout the cutting and edge-rounding processes.

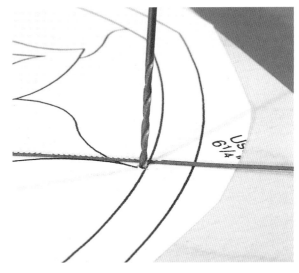

2–14. Drilling a 1/32-inch entry hole for a No. 2 blade to one side of an inside border piece line.

2–15. Sawing technique for cutting a parallel line to a curved or straight edge. The two stationary fingers of the left hand act as contact points and a cutting guide while the stock is advanced with the right hand to complete the curved portion of the cut.

Sawing is best done whenever possible with a No. 2 blade, even when cutting material ¼ to ¾ inch in thickness. A No. 2 blade cuts a very narrow kerf and any gaps between sawn segments will be almost totally eliminated when

2–16. An auxiliary zero clearance table keeps all small parts from falling through the regular opening of the saw table.

the segments and their edges are coated with paint and finally glued in place.

Reducing Workpiece Thicknesses

Reducing the thicknesses of sawn segments and background pieces is often required so some areas of the work may project outward from others to be in relief. Relief on project surfaces can be achieved by either placing prepared shims under certain pieces or reducing the thicknesses of others. Thicknesses can be reduced

with belt- or disc-sanding machines or by sawing with a band saw or scroll saw. Since many segments are of relatively small size and much too dangerous to machine, especially with the band saw, scroll-saw resawing is the best method.

Resawing small segments with a scroll saw can be done freehand or with the aid of a shop-made fence accessory. When resawing, with or without the fence, it is always helpful to mark the edges all around each part, indicating how much material needs to be removed. This is easily accomplished using a finger-gauging technique (**2–17**) or with a shop-made "scribbing" jig (**2–18**). Illus. **2–19** provides a full-size cutting and drilling pattern that can be permanently glued to a block of hardwood (**2–20** and **2–21**).

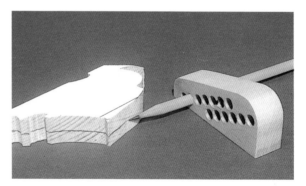

2–18. A shop-made scribbing jig in use.

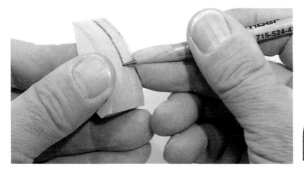

2–17. Finger-gauging a guideline for reducing the thickness of a workpiece.

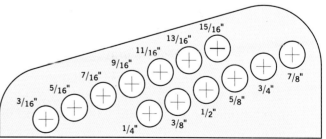

2–19. Full-size pattern for a scribbing jig. Drill the hole size to match pencil.

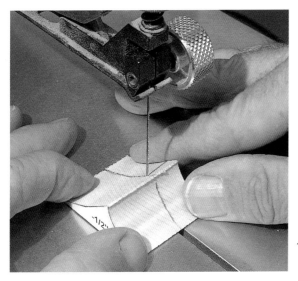

2–20. Freehand resawing a small part on the scroll saw to reduce its thickness.

Bandsaw Resawing

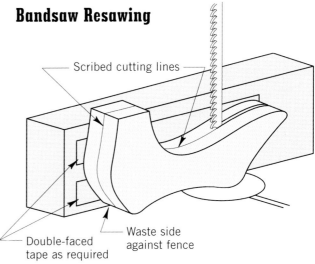

Scribed cutting lines

Waste side against fence

Double-faced tape as required

2–21. Freehand resawing of medium- to larger-sized pieces can be done on a band saw using this technique which keeps fingers at a safe distance.

The shop-made scroll-saw ripping/resawing fixture has a fence permanently secured to a auxiliary table (2–22 to 2–26). Because most scroll-saw blades, like band-saw blades, tend to track slightly to one side, the feed direction may need to be slightly angular to compensate for the lead. Review the setup procedures as explained for setting up a resawing fence for the band saw as described under Technique No. 2 on *pages 19* and *20* (2–25).

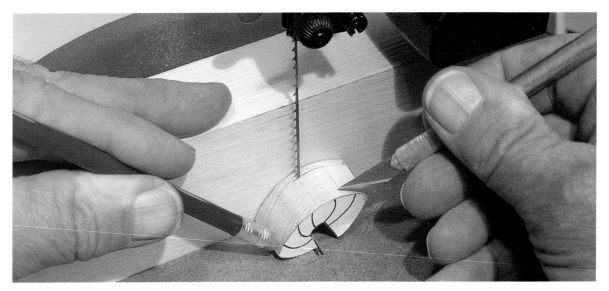

2–22. Resawing small parts using the scroll saw with a combination resawing fence and auxiliary table. Notice the use of a "thick wood" cutting blade.

Rounding Over and Shaping

After all of the parts of an intarsia project have been cut out and those to be reduced or resawn to thickness have been attended to, it's time to round over the edges. Remember to leave the patterns attached as long as possible. If you have removed stock from the faces of some segments, it may be helpful to mark the back surfaces with an X to keep all of the front surfaces properly oriented.

The majority of projects require removing just a minimum of material from the face edges of each segment in the rounding-over process. The actual radius or chamfer is usually only about $\frac{1}{32}$ to $\frac{1}{16}$ inch, which, in most situations, can be worked by hand with 80- to 120-grit sheet abrasives (**2–27** and **2–28**). This leaves about an $\frac{1}{8}$-inch-wide indent all along the lines between two adjoining segments. Larger projects could have a slightly wider indent. Use a high-speed rotary tool for the fastest and best results.

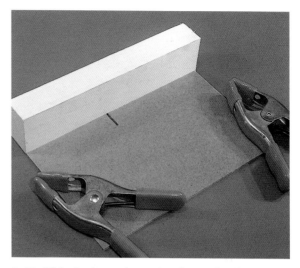

2–23. This ripping and resawing fixture for the scroll saw is easy to make.

Small sanding drums (**2–29**), structured carbide cutters (**2–30**), and diamond burrs (**2–31**) must be moved over the edges quickly with a fairly rapid, back-and-forth action and very little pressure. Use a very light and quick rubbing action. A hesitation or slow feed with

Bandsaw Resawing Fence

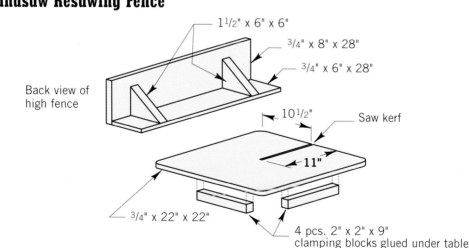

Back view of high fence

$1\frac{1}{2}$" x 6" x 6"

$\frac{3}{4}$" x 8" x 28"

$\frac{3}{4}$" x 6" x 28"

$10\frac{1}{2}$"

Saw kerf

11"

$\frac{3}{4}$" x 22" x 22"

4 pcs. 2" x 2" x 9" clamping blocks glued under table

2–24. Details for making a scroll saw ripping/resawing fixture.

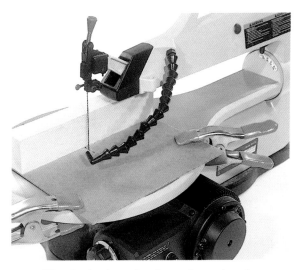

2–25. The ripping/resawing fence clamped to the scroll-saw table.

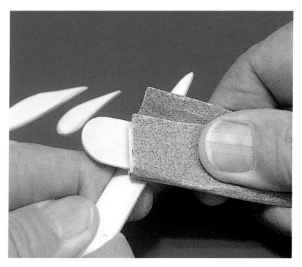

2–27. An abrasive sheet wrapped around a tongue depressor makes a good rounding-over tool.

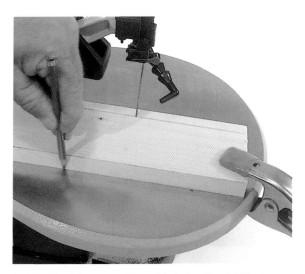

2–28. Rounding over straight edges of a workpiece with sandpaper held flat on the workbench surface.

2–26. Checking a scroll-saw blade for "lead." Notice the blade in the cutting line (drawn in red) parallel to the right edge of the board, which is held in place with the power off. A line parallel to the cut is now drawn onto the surface of the saw table. The ripping/resawing fence will be clamped parallel to this line as shown in 2-25.

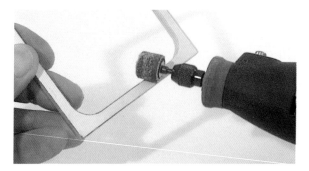

2–29. Using a small drum sander in a high-speed rotary tool to round the inside edge of a frame piece.

2–30. A structured carbide cutter in a rotary tool removes material quickly.

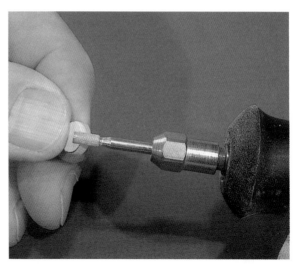

2–31. Very small pieces are safely and quickly rounded over using diamond-coated microburrs. See Illus. 1-9 on page 13.

2–32. Properly applied patterns should remove easily; otherwise, use appropriate solvents to soften the adhesive.

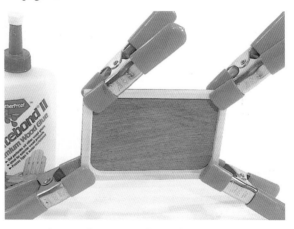

2–33. Gluing a frame to a plywood backer.

the tool engaged on the work will result in a deep cut and an uneven edge. Illus. **2–31** shows a pretty straightforward technique for rounding over the edges of very small segments. *Tip:* If diamond burrs or sanding drums load up with pitch or resin, they can be cleaned by running the tool against an "abrasive cleaning stick" of the type used to clean and renew belt and disc sanders. The residue on diamond and/or

structured carbide cutters can be burned off with a torch.

Coarse-grit sanding drums and structured carbide cutters should be used only to remove greater amounts of material. This type of power cutting is ideal for shaping various surfaces.

Final smoothing and sanding work should require minimum effort, if any. The diamond microburrs can be used to smooth surfaces

2–34. Painting the frame/border piece with acrylic craft paint. Coat all visible edges and only the rear surface of the backer.

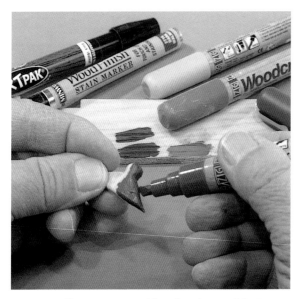

2–35. Small pieces are quickly colored using felt-tip markers.

initially rounded over with coarser-grit sanding drums and/or coarser structured carbide cutters. Remove any patterns or pattern pieces still attached to the wood (2–32). If too much adhesive, or the wrong kind, was used, soften the adhesive with lacquer thinner or mineral spirits.

Painting and Assembly

Projects having integral frames are best prepared by gluing the frame piece to the backer first (2–33). When the glue has cured, paint the frame and its outside edges (2–34). Refer to the project photos for recommended paint color and finish selections. Water-based paints or felt-tip markers (2–35 and 2–36) are recommended for coloring small parts because of

2–36. Stained and colored pieces ready to be glued to a backer.

2–38. Applying the second color in an acrylic sponge finish employing a "dabbing" action.

2–37. Close-up showing a finish applied by sponge to various colored pieces of a project.

their ease of use. A very light sanding may be necessary to remove all raised fibers. For stained projects, it is suggested that water-based stains be considered.

Sponge Finishes

Multiple color finishes such as that shown in 2–37 will be needed on some projects. These finishes are easier to create than they look. Simply apply a base coat of a selected color. Then use small pieces of sponge (premoistened with water for acrylic paints) and dab on the second or third colors, making a random pattern (2–38).

Backers

As a general rule, use thick backers when possible, especially when making large projects. Thin and unfinished backers have greater tendencies to warp. The backers to which the

2–39. This photo illustrates how the background pieces have been reduced in thickness to create a dimensional face. Also shown is a project with a square, and visible, thick-edge, painted backer the same size as the project's dimensions.

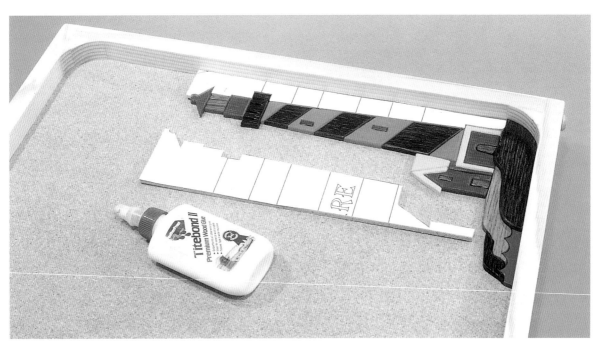

2–40. Sometimes the individual parts are glued or overlaid onto a large panel, thus eliminating the need for a typical backer.

various cut, shaped, and finished pieces are glued to, may or may not be visible in the finished project (**2–39** to **2–41**). Sometimes, square or rectangular straight-edge projects, such as those used for box lids, may be painted and actually have their edges visible. In this case, a high-quality plywood such as Baltic birch with its void-free plys should be used.

In general, backers made for intarsia projects with irregular profiles are, as a rule, not as visible. They are cut about ⅛ to ¼ inch smaller all around (**2–41**) and may or may not have their edges beveled back.

Special Techniques

Individual creative expression in shaping and painting is encouraged. Additional detailing, for example, can be achieved by just painting a white dot on an eye, using a wood-burning tool to groove and texture surfaces or to add definition lines on unpainted wood surfaces, and so on. Remember to sign each piece you make (**2–42**). Complete each project with the application of a clear, satin acrylic-spray top coat. Always apply at least two or more coats of finish to the backer. This will reduce warpage tendencies which are present because of unbalanced construction. Add a saw-tooth wall hanger to the back of the project or install other hardware as necessary.

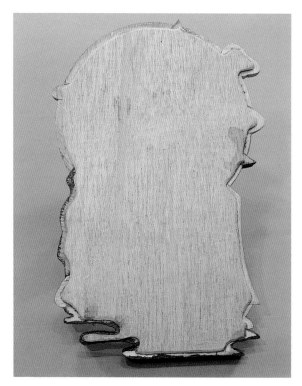

2–41. This rear view shows a backer made from recycled plywood wall paneling that is cut slightly smaller than the face profile and has beveled edges.

2–42. Sign the project so your work can be identified in the future.

CHAPTER 3

Flat Projects

This chapter provides 24 projects with similar construction details. The major difference between the projects is that while most have integral frames worked into the design, some do not (3–1). All of the designs are flat, meaning that there are no individual segments set out from the others in relief. Relief features, however, can easily be created by simply inserting thin shims under selected areas of the pattern or reducing the background thickness of pieces surrounding the main subject.

The designs and patterns that follow can be enlarged to any size desired. If used for wall hangings, for example, they can be sized to fit a specific space or need. And in addition to wall hangings, the flat designs in this chapter are easily incorporated into furniture designs such as tabletop inlays, cabinets, and chest doors or panels. Many of the designs can be interchanged with those shown in the functional projects in Chapter 5.

Smaller designs with straight or irregular edges can be used as lids of box covers. Other designs can be used as overlays glued onto larger panels such as mirrors, bulletin boards, or clock faces. Also, consider the possibilities of utilizing only partial details or areas of a design pattern, by picking out a key element and eliminating the remaining background features.

The facing material thickness can range from ⅛- to ¼-inch plywood for almost any size project. Small- to medium-sized projects can be made from solid wood ⅛ to ¼ inch thick, but good stock selection, careful preparation, and proper finishing techniques are required to minimize wood warpage tendencies.

Once you have the pattern sized and the material prepared, follow these simple steps:

1. Cut out all the project pieces as per the pattern using a No. 2 reverse-tooth or 2/0 scroll-saw blade.

2. Round over the sawn edges to a ½₃₂- to ¹⁄₁₆-inch radius.

3. Sand and paint the face surfaces and edge of all pieces.

4. Glue frame pieces to the backer first and then glue the painted segments to the backer.

Refer to Chapter 2 for more detailed and illustrated instructional techniques. Use the photo provided with each project to assist with color and finishing selections.

Stars & Stripes

Below: Stars & Stripes.
Bottom: Pattern for Stars & Stripes.

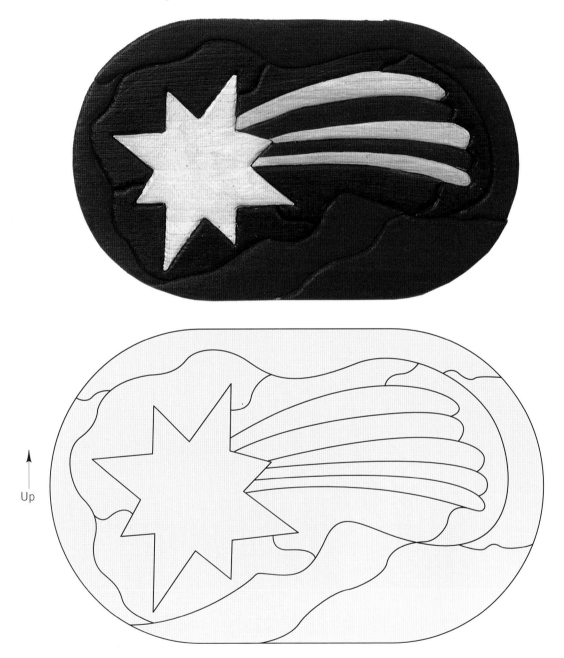

Up

Full-size pattern or size to suit.
Use $1/4"$ or $3/8"$ stock ($3^1/4"$ x $5^3/8"$) and $1/8"$ plywood backer.

Masai Shield

Below left: Masai Shield.
Below right: Pattern for Masai Shield.

Full-size pattern or change to suit.
Use 1/4" material and 1/8" plywood backer.

Concrete Truck

Below: Concrete Truck.

Bottom: Pattern for Concrete Truck.

Size pattern to suit.

Use 1/4" material and 1/8" plywood backer.

Turtle Party Guy

Right: Turtle Party Guy.
See page 38 for the pattern.

Abstract

Right: Abstract.
See page 39 for the pattern.

Turtle Party Guy

Full-size pattern or size to suit.
Use ¹/₄" by 6³/₄" x 7³/₄" material with a ¹/₄" plywood backer.

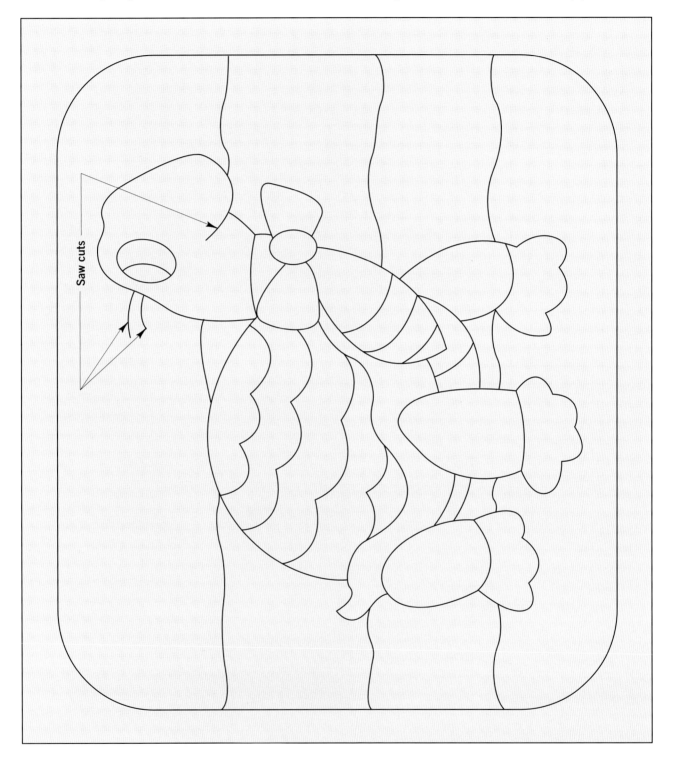

Abstract

Full-size pattern or size to suit.
Use $1/4$" by 6 $3/4$" x 7 $3/4$" material with a $1/4$" plywood backer.

Swordfish

Below: Swordfish.
Facing page: Pattern for Swordfish.

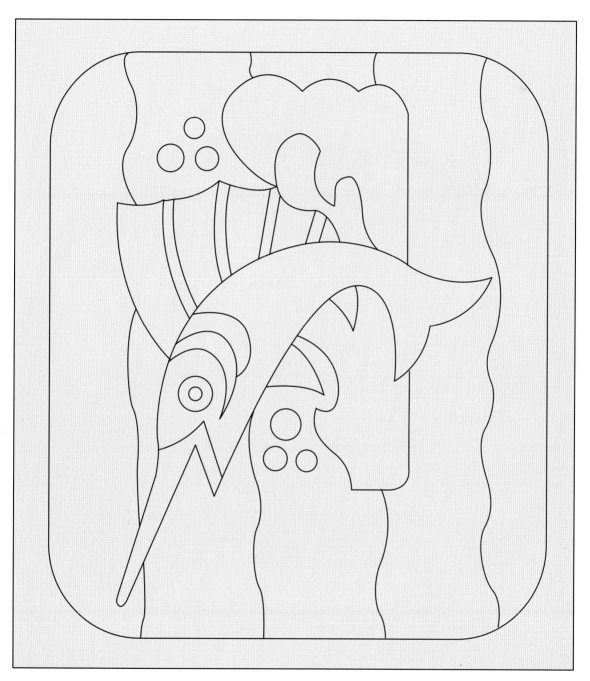

Swordfish

Enlarge pattern 110% or size to suit.
Use $1/4$" x 7" x 8" material with $1/8$" plywood backer.

Gargoyle Head

Below: Gargoyle Head.
Facing page: Pattern for Gargoyle Head.

Size pattern to suit.
Use $1/4"$ material and $1/4"$ plywood backer.

Gargoyle Head

Horse Gargoyle

Below: Horse Gargoyle.
Facing page: Pattern for Horse Gargoyle.

Horse Gargoyle

Size pattern to suit.
Use 1/4" material and 1/4" plywood backer.

Dachshund Quilt

Below: Dachshund Quilt.
Facing page: Pattern for Dachshund Quilt.

Enlarge pattern 125%.
Use $1/4$" x $10^1/4$" x $7^3/4$" stock and $1/4$" plywood backer.

Dachshund Quilt

Moonscape

Below: Moonscape.

Facing page: Pattern for Moonscape.

Moonscape

Full-size pattern or size to suit.
Use $1/4$" x $61/4$" x $73/4$" stock and a $1/4$" plywood backer.

Cape Cod Lighthouse

Below: Cape Cod Lighthouse.
Facing page: Pattern for Cape Cod Lighthouse.

Cape Cod Lighthouse

Size pattern to suit.
Use $1/4$" material and $1/4$" plywood backer.

Maple Leaf Quilt

Below: Maple Leaf Quilt.
Facing page: Pattern for Maple Leaf Quilt.

Maple Leaf Quilt

Full-size pattern or size to suit.
Use $1/4$" x $6 1/4$" x $7 3/4$" stock with a $1/4$" plywood backer.

House and Pine-Tree Quilt

Below: House and Pine-Tree Quilt.

Facing page: Pattern for House and Pine-Tree Quilt.

House and Pine-Tree Quilt

Size pattern to suit.
Use $1/4$" material and $1/4$" plywood backer.

Nutcracker Guard

Below: Nutcracker Guard.
Facing page: Pattern for Nutcracker Guard.

Nutcracker Guard

Full-size pattern or size to suit.

Use $3/8$" stock with $1/8$" plywood backer.

Paint eyeball and other face details.

Futuristic Scene

Below: Futuristic Scene.

Facing page: Pattern for Futuristic Scene.

Futuristic Scene

Size pattern to suit.
Use 1/4" material and 1/4" plywood backer.

Native-American Design

Below: Native-American Design.

Facing page: Pattern for Native-American Design.

Native-American Design

Full-size pattern or size to suit.
Use $1/4$" x $6 1/2$" square material and $1/8$" plywood backer.

Carousel Horse

Below: Carousel Horse.

Facing page: Pattern for Carousel Horse.

Carousel Horse

Full-size pattern or size to suit.
Use $1/4$" x $6 3/4$" x $7 5/8$" stock with a $1/4$" plywood backer.

Pop Relaxing

Below: Pop Relaxing.
Facing page: Pattern for Pop Relaxing.

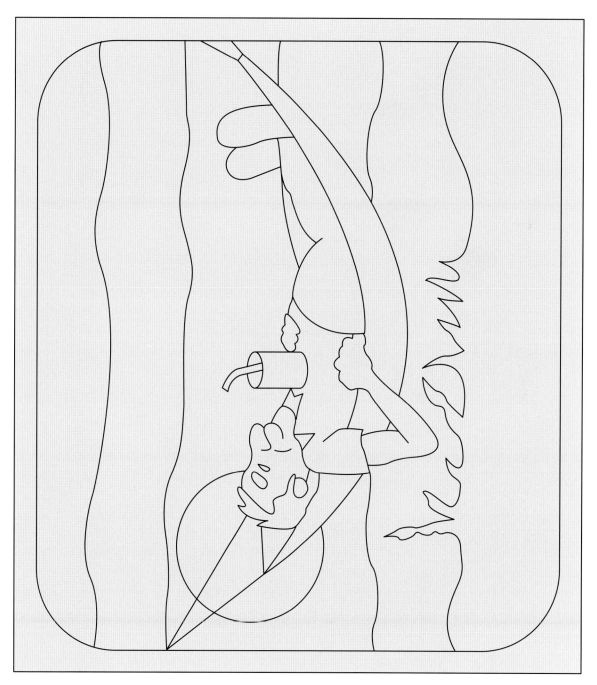

Pop Relaxing

Size pattern to suit.
Use 1/4" stock with 1/8" or 1/4" plywood backer.

Pop at the Beach

Below: Pop at the Beach.
Facing page: Pattern for Pop at the Beach.

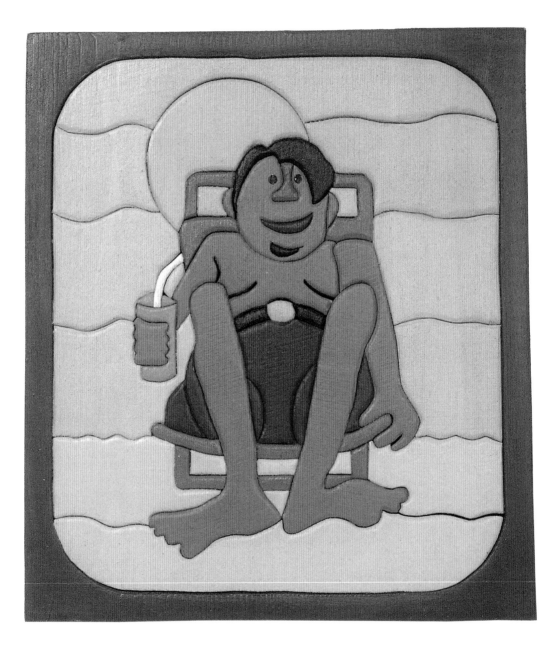

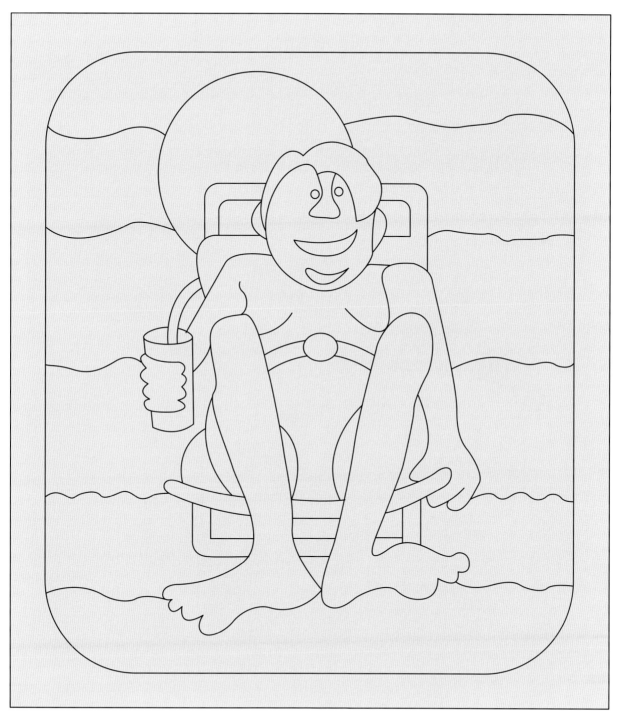

Pop at the Beach

Size pattern to suit.
Use $1/4$" material and $1/4$" plywood backer.

Lazy Fisherman

Below: Lazy Fisherman.
Facing page: Pattern for Lazy Fisherman.

Lazy Fisherman

Size pattern to suit.
Use ¼" material and ¼" plywood backer.

Stylized Butterfly

Below: Stylized Butterfly.
Facing page: Pattern for Stylized Butterfly.

Full-size pattern or size to suit.
Use $1/4$" material and $1/4$" plywood backer.

Stylized Butterfly

Old-Time Sailing Ship

Below: Old-Time Sailing Ship.
Facing page: Pattern for Old-Time Sailing Ship.

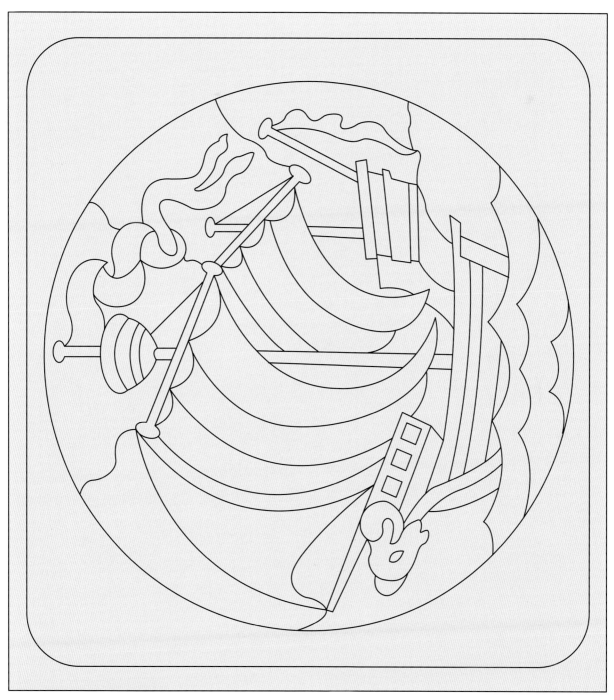

Old-Time Sailing Ship

Full-size pattern or size to suit.
Use $1/4$" x $6 3/4$" x $7 3/8$" stock with $1/4$" plywood backer.

Iris

Below: Iris.
Facing page: Pattern for Iris.

Iris

Size pattern to suit.
Use $1/4$" material and $1/4$" plywood backer.

Fast Car

Below: Fast Car.

Facing page: Pattern for Fast Car.

Fast Car
Design by Brian Dahlen

Size pattern to suit.

Note: Use $3/8"$ or $1/4"$ material to overlay design pieces onto $1/4"$ plywood panel with optional frame.

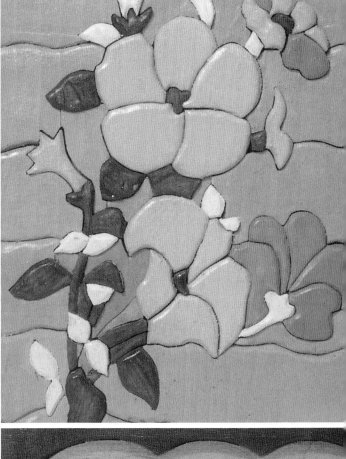

CHAPTER 4

Dimensional Intarsia Projects

The projects featured in this chapter have some relief, which makes their surfaces more dimensional and visually interesting. This effect is easily achieved by either reducing the thicknesses of selected pieces or shimming others. One popular technique is to reduce the thicknesses of the background pieces, leaving the subject parts or major features to stand out in relief.

Some projects in this chapter have multiple levels or thicknesses. The patterns provide some

Kachina Face with solid woods cut to fit around the face.
See pages 88 and 89.

instructions. A plus (+) symbol with a fraction indicates the amount a piece should be elevated. In most cases, however, it is faster and easier to simply reduce the thicknesses of background pieces instead of cutting numerous shims needed to elevate cut-out letters, for example. The patterns or instructions for these projects will indicate a minus (-) designation. Parts without either a plus or minus designation are left at the thickness used when starting the project.

Happy and Sad Faces

Below: Two projects: one showing a happy face, and the other a sad one. The happy face has all the white areas reduced ⅛ inch. So does the sad face, except for the white triangular piece in the forehead.

Facing page: Patterns for the Happy and Sad Faces.

Happy and Sad Faces

Full-size patterns or size to suit.
Use $3/8$" or $1/2$" material and $1/8$" plywood backers.
Reduce face background thickness $1/8$".

Dolphin

Below: Dolphin. Not reducing the perimeter background pieces creates a frame-like effect.

Facing page: Pattern for Dolphin.

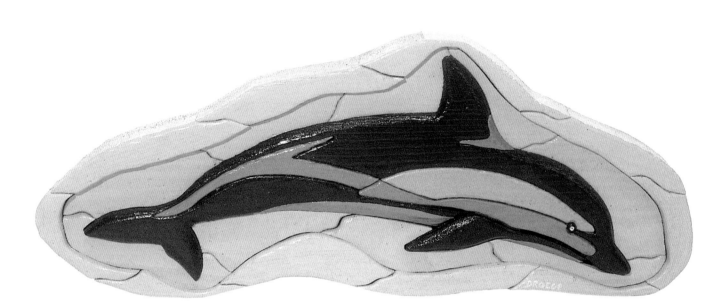

Dolphin

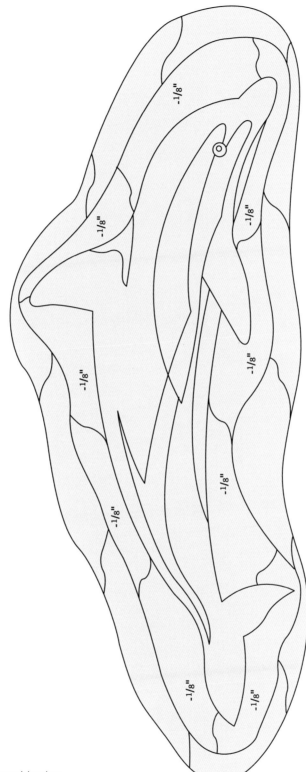

Size pattern as desired.

Use $3/4$" material and $1/8$" plywood backer.

Folk-Art Flower

Below: Folk-Art Flower. This project has a frameless, irregular edge.

Facing page: Pattern for Folk-Art Flower.

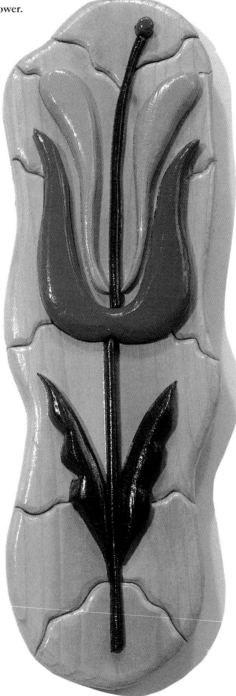

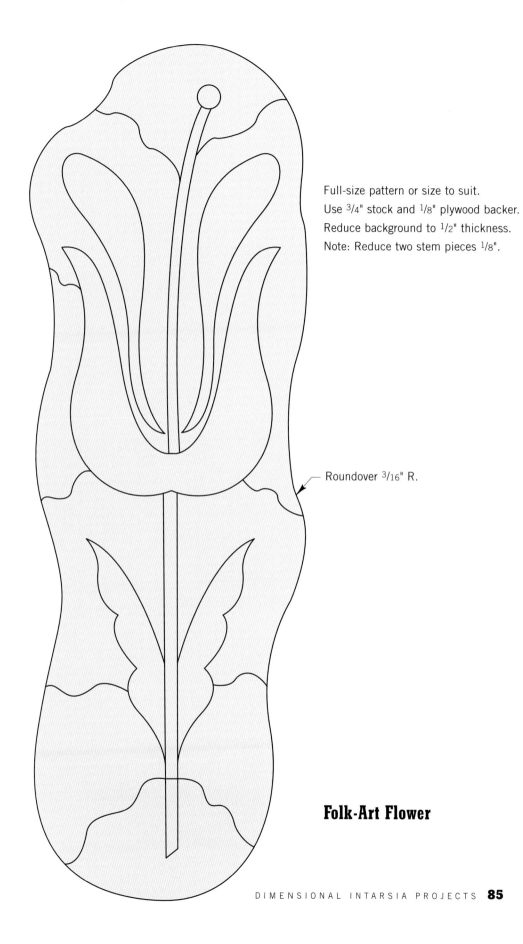

Full-size pattern or size to suit.
Use $3/4$" stock and $1/8$" plywood backer.
Reduce background to $1/2$" thickness.
Note: Reduce two stem pieces $1/8$".

Roundover $3/16$" R.

Folk-Art Flower

Radiation Abstract

Below: Radiation Abstract. This is a typical intarsia project made from numerous pieces of ¾-inch scrap wood, each fit carefully together and all at the same level with the exception of the star, which is shimmed ⅛ inch.

Facing page: Pattern for Radiation Abstract.

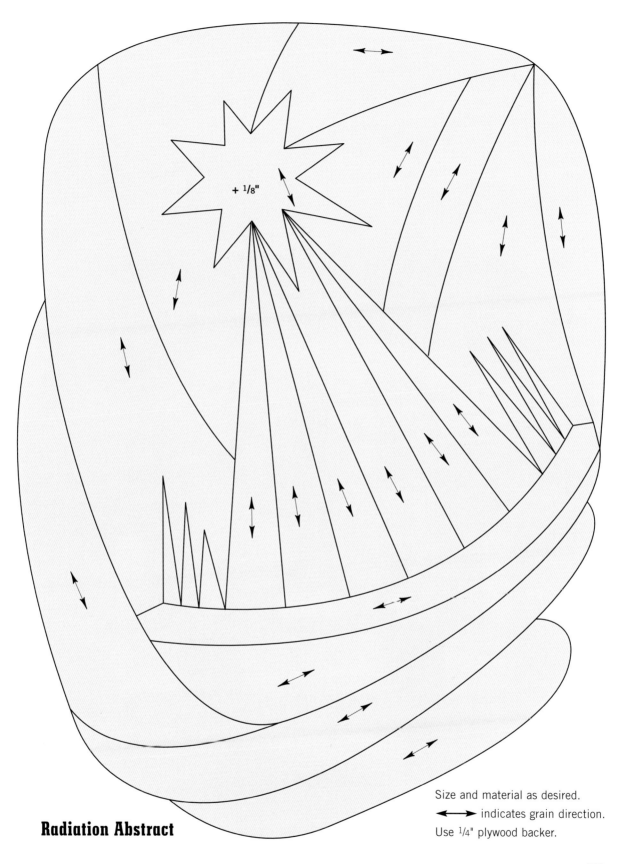

+ 1/8"

Radiation Abstract

Size and material as desired.
⟷ indicates grain direction.
Use 1/4" plywood backer.

Kachina Face

Below: Kachina Face. All stained pieces are ¼-inch thick solid woods and are cut to fit around the face.

Facing page: Pattern for Kachina Face.

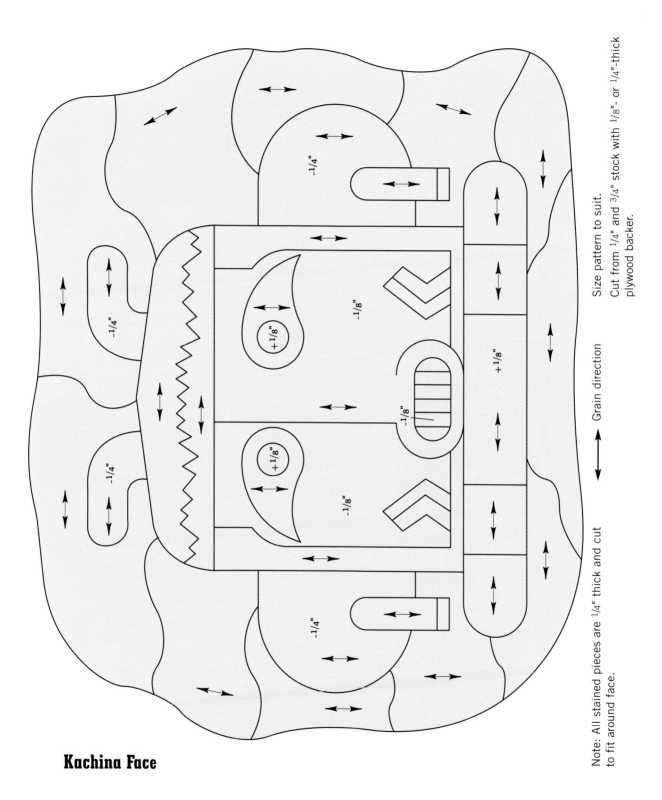

Kachina Face

Size pattern to suit.

Cut from 1/4" and 3/4" stock with 1/8"- or 1/4"-thick plywood backer.

Grain direction

Note: All stained pieces are 1/4" thick and cut to fit around face.

Stylized Fish

Below: Stylized Fish, cut from ¾-inch solid wood.

Right: View showing reduced background pieces and well-rounded outside edges of the fish and its multiple levels.

Facing page: Pattern for Stylized Fish.

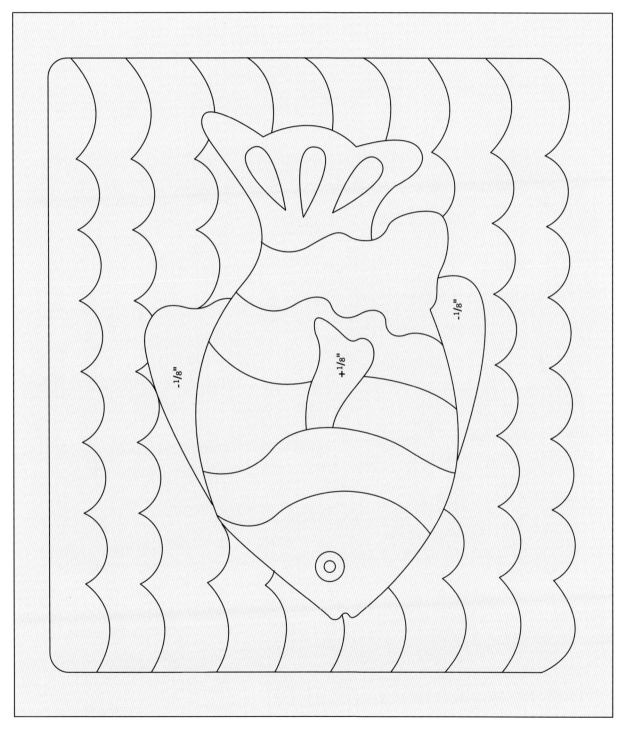

Full-size pattern.

Use 3/4" x 63/4" x 71/2" stock and 1/4" plywood backer.

Reduce back-ground pieces to 1/2" thickness.

Shape chest and tail pieces before cutting into seg-ments.

Paint pupil of eye piece.

-1/8"

+1/8"

-1/8"

Stylized Fish

Queen of the Holsteins

Below: Queen of the Holsteins. This project features three different levels of background/thickness reductions.

Facing page: Pattern for Queen of the Holsteins.

Queen of the Holsteins

Size pattern to suit.
Use 3/4" material and 1/4" plywood backer.
Reduce sky thickness 1/4".
Reduce farm and hills 3/16".
Reduce foreground, tail, udder, and far side legs 1/8".

Socrates' Quotation

Below: Socrates' Quotation. This project is cut from ¾-inch-thick solid wood, with the background pieces reduced ⅛ inch.

Facing page, top: Pattern for Socrates' Quotation.

Facing page, bottom: A close look at the letter work.

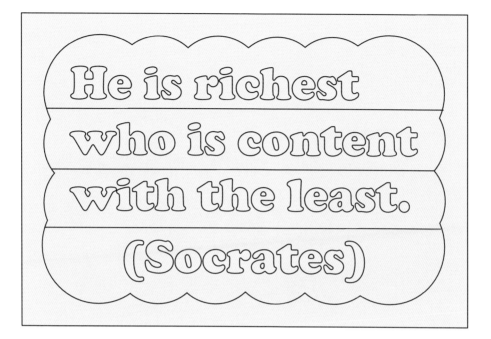

Socrates' Quotation

Enlarge 200% or size pattern to suit.
Use $3/4$" material and $1/4$" plywood backer.
Reduce background pieces $1/8$".

Raised Sign

Below: Raised Sign.

Facing page: Pattern for the Raised Sign.

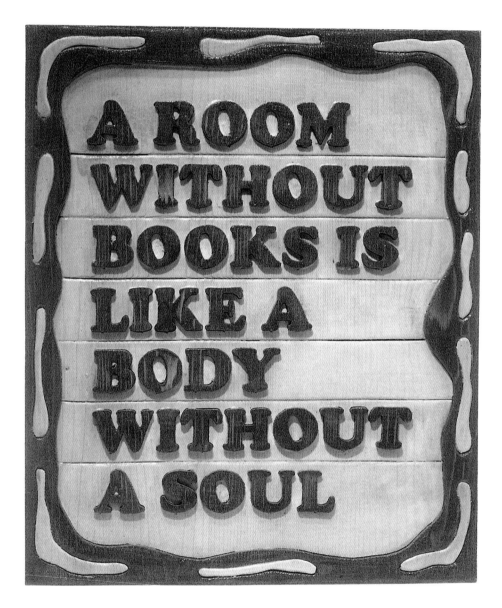

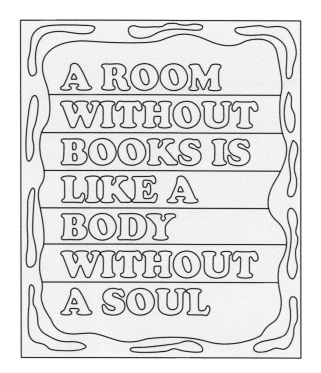

Raised Sign

Enlarge 200 to 250% or size pattern to suit.
Use $3/4$" material and $1/4$" plywood backer.
Reduce background pieces $1/8$".

Memories

Below: Memories. Raised lettering and raised art are easily created by reducing background thickness.

Right: This edge view shows ¾-inch solid wood with a ¼-inch plywood backer cut square and flush to the edge.

Facing page: Pattern for Memories.

Memories

Enlarge pattern 125% or size pattern to suit.
Use $3/4"$ stock, $7^3/4"$ x $10^1/4"$, with $1/4"$ plywood backer.
Reduce all background pieces $1/8"$.

Wildflowers

Below: Wildflowers.

Facing page: Pattern for Wildflowers.

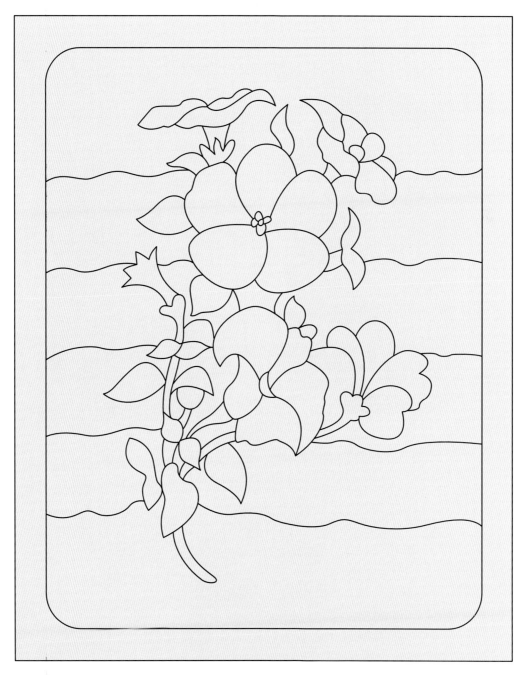

Wildflowers

Full-size pattern or size to suit.
Use $1/4$" material and $1/4$" plywood backer.
Reduce background pieces $1/8$".

Lighthouse and Boat

Below left and right: Stained and painted versions of the Lighthouse and Boat.

Bottom: An angular view shows relief.

Facing page: Pattern for Lighthouse and Boat.

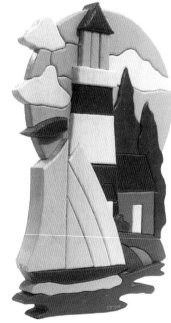

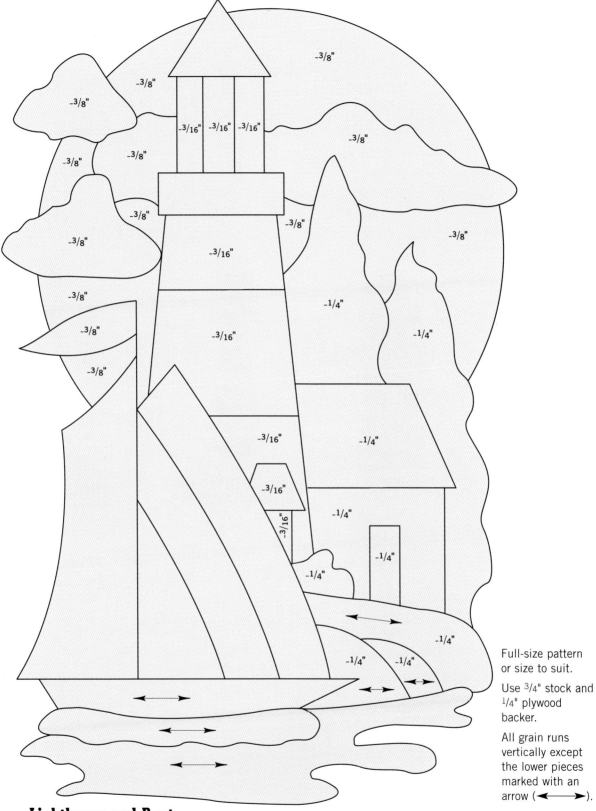

−3/8"

−3/8"

−3/8"

−3/8"

−3/8"

−3/16" −3/16" −3/16"

−3/8"

−3/8"

−3/8"

−3/8"

−3/8"

−3/8"

−3/8"

−3/8"

−3/8"

−3/16"

−3/16"

−1/4"

−1/4"

−3/16"

−1/4"

−3/16"

−3/16"

−1/4"

−1/4"

−1/4"

−1/4"

−1/4"

−1/4"

−1/4"

Full-size pattern
or size to suit.

Use 3/4" stock and
1/4" plywood
backer.

All grain runs
vertically except
the lower pieces
marked with an
arrow (◄——►).

Lighthouse and Boat

3-D Lighthouses

This fun-filled project requires some bevel-sawing procedures to cut the stackable tower and base pieces (**A** to **E**). The most tricky is part "**A**," the very top piece. First, drill the dowel hole about ½ inch deep. Next, make the cut with a left table tilt at 45 degrees and a counter-clockwise workpiece feed into the blade as shown in **E**. Use a no. 5 or no. 7 skip-tooth blade, not the more aggressive ground-tip blades. It may be necessary to consider your first try as just a practice run. Once you get the feel of the feeding requirements and the pivoting technique, it is an easy cut.

Painted and stained 3-D Lighthouses
with slightly different bases.

A few parts of this three-dimensional project involve fundamental intarsia techniques, and it is a fun project to make. See pages 106 and 107 for the patterns.

A protractor used on the table makes setting the amount of table tilt for bevel-sawing easy.

Bevel-sawing the top piece at 45 degrees creates this cone-shaped piece.

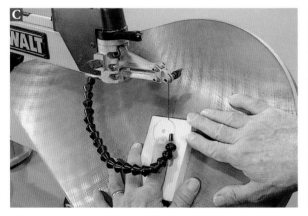

The cut is made with the table tilted left and a careful counterclockwise feed while rotating the piece on its center.

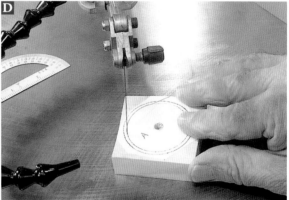

Cutting the lower tower pieces at a 5-degree bevel employing a clockwise feed and following the inside line.

Making all of the other five-degree bevel-edge tower pieces (**D**) is not nearly as tricky. They may be cut with either a clockwise or counterclockwise feed. Just be sure to follow the correct pattern lines and work on the correct side of the blade.

The small compound-sawn boat is optional. If necessary, refer to *The New Scroll Saw Handbook* for more information regarding this technique.

Painting or staining and assembly is pretty straightforward.

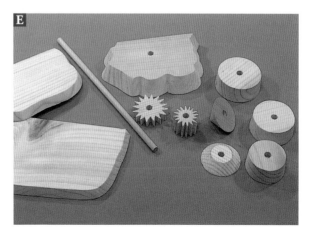

The base and some of the cut-out tower pieces.

3-D Lighthouses

Patterns for tower.

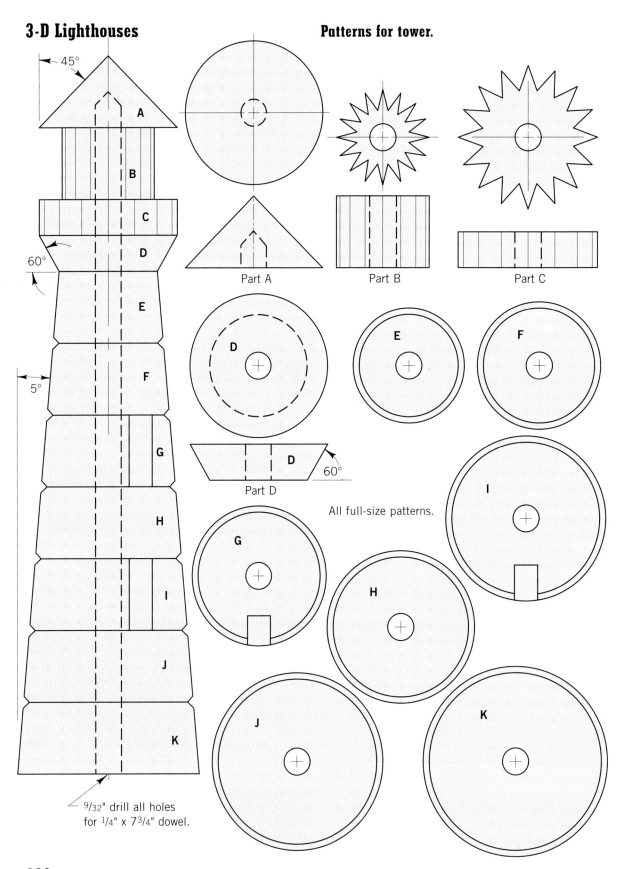

45°

A

B

C

D

60°

E

F

5°

G

H

I

J

K

9/32" drill all holes
for 1/4" x 7 3/4" dowel.

Part A

Part B

Part C

D

E

F

I

D

60°

Part D

All full-size patterns.

G

H

K

J

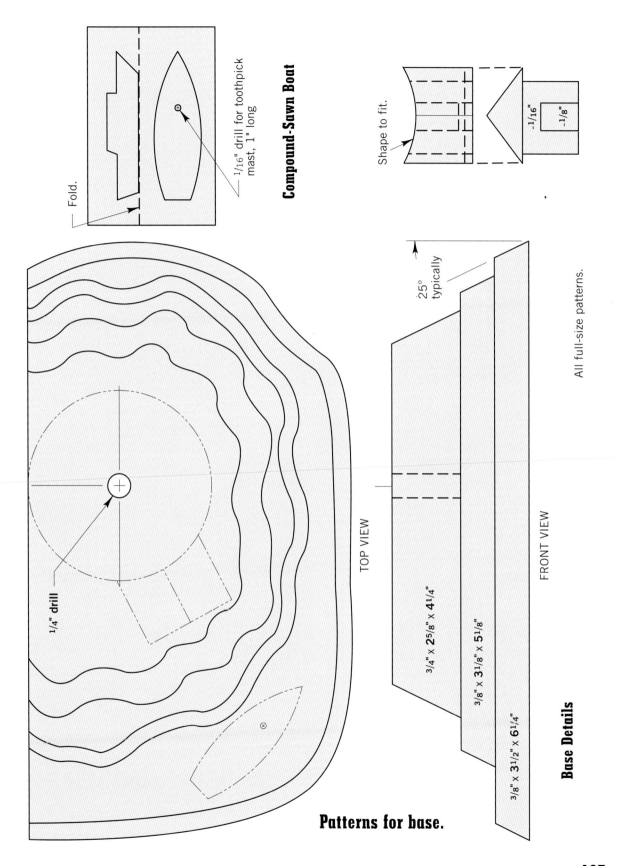

Compound-Sawn Boat

Fold.

¹/₁₆" drill for toothpick mast, 1" long

Shape to fit.

-1/16"

-1/8"

25° typically

All full-size patterns.

TOP VIEW

FRONT VIEW

¹/₄" drill

³/₄" x 2⁵/₈" x 4¹/₄"

³/₈" x 3¹/₈" x 5¹/₈"

³/₈" x 3¹/₂" x 6¹/₄"

Base Details

Patterns for base.

CHAPTER 5

Functional Projects

Almost all of the designs in this chapter can be used to make some type of useful item. Many designs, for example, can be enlarged to a size suitable for an entire tabletop, or simply used as an inlay within it. The intarsia pieces shown in these projects can be interchanged with many of the designs previously illustrated.

Every attempt was made to include the most fundamental project construction details and techniques. All projects are made using inexpensive pine and simple joinery which can be upgraded or modified as desired. Simple-to-execute inlaying techniques are included that involve common scroll-sawing and routing techniques. Due to limited space, we recommend *The New Scroll Saw Handbook* and *The New Router Handbook* if additional instructional information is required.

The project descriptions that follow provide essential fabrication details and also suggest other designs and patterns from this book that can be substituted. Patterns will need to be sized appropriately.

Examples of functional projects (clockwise from upper left): Dragon Wall Cabinet, Folk-Art Flowers Paper-Towel Holder, Hanging Flowers Inlay Table, and Tropical Fish Mantle Clock.

Simple Butterfly Napkin/Letter Holder

This project features a flush inlay technique employing a bevel-cutting operation with a scroll saw. The photo below shows a "near flush" inlay in which the butterfly intarsia piece is about 1/32 to 1/16 inch elevated above the background. This is done to distinguish the inlay from being perceived or viewed as just a flat design painted onto the surface. As an alternative technique to inlaying, simply cut this intarsia inlay from 1/16- to 1/8-inch Baltic plywood and glue the finished pieces onto the surfaces(s).

The black outline of this intarsia piece ensures that the inlay visually blends in if it doesn't fit perfectly into the recess of a light background. Make the butterfly from 1/4- and 1/8-inch plywood (face and backer) and finish it as separate pieces, as shown in **A**. Trace its outline profile onto the side piece(s) as a scroll-saw bevel-cutting line. Tilt the table to the appropriate angle (3½ to 5 degrees) that works with the blade selected. Make test cuts on scrap. Illustrations **A** and **B** show that the angular cut will pinch the butterfly profile cutout as it is pushed inward, creating a recess on the face side and an elevation on the rear (inside) surface.

Consider these alternate designs: Stars & Stripes *(page 34)*, Swordfish *(page 40)*, Native-American Design *(page 60)*, and Stylized Fish *(page 90)*.

This basic project provides good surfaces for inlaying or overlaying small intarsia designs. See pages 112 and 113 for the patterns.

A thin plywood intarsia piece is made, painted, and then traced onto a side piece so a recess can be bevel scroll-sawn in the surface.

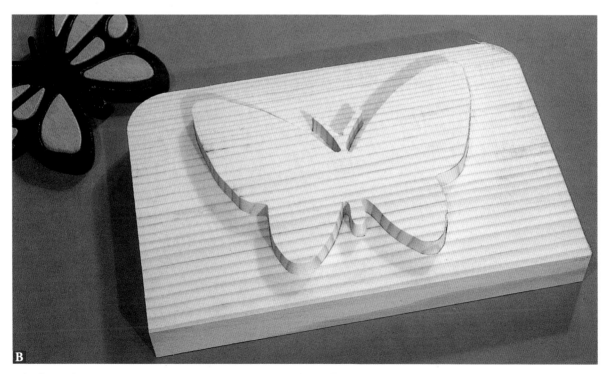

The face-side recess creates an elevation on the rear (inside) surface that must be planed or sanded off.

Simple Butterfly

Size pattern to suit.
Use $1/4$" material and $1/8$" plywood backer.

Napkin/Letter Holder

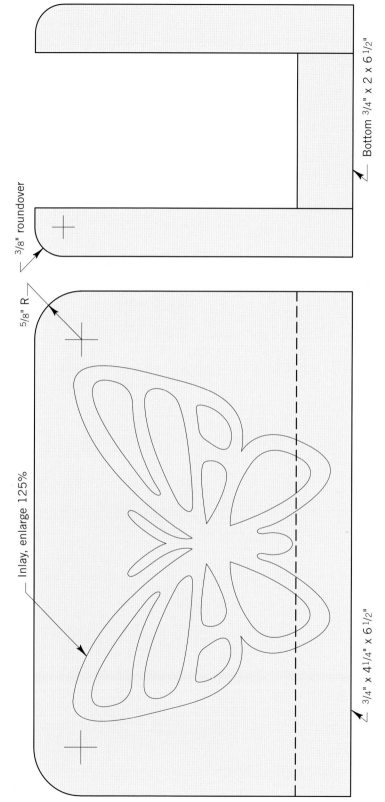

Bottom 3/4" x 2 x 6 1/2"

3/8" roundover

5/8" R

Inlay, enlarge 125%

3/4" x 4 1/4" x 6 1/2"

Pennsylvania Dutch Hex Design Inlaid Plate

Inlaying round intarsia designs into a purchased wooden plate makes a stunning project. Basswood plates with plain or scalloped edges as shown below are available in sizes from 6 to 14 inches in diameter from craft supply sources. Oval, octagonal, and rectangular plate or tray shapes are also available. These are commonly used for chip-carving, wood-burning, and country- or tole-painting projects.

Generally, the procedure is to make the intarsia inlay as a separate project, as shown on the facing page. When finished, trace the profile onto the plate with a sharp pencil or a knife edge. Then cut through the plate with the scroll saw. Apply instant, or heavy, gap-filling glue to hold the inlay in place. An alternate, and the best, installation technique is to use a lathe or a router to machine a recess cut to a suitable depth.

Refer to the Swordfish *(page 40)*, Native-American Design *(page 60)*, Old-Time Sailing Ship *(page 72)*, Stylized Fish *(page 90)*, and Hanging Flowers Inlaid Table *(page 148)* for other intarsia designs suitable for plate and tray inlay projects.

Colorful intarsia pieces inlaid into purchased wooden plates and trays commonly used for various crafts make eye-catching projects.

Make the inlay piece separately.

Enlarge pattern 105% or size to suit.

Use $1/4"$ x 7" square material with a $1/4"$ plywood backer.

Pennsylvania Dutch Hex Design

Cape Lookout Lighthouse Box

This project is just one example of how attractive boxes can easily be made using colorful square or rectangular intarsia lids. The intarsia piece should be made of ¼-inch material with a ¼-inch plywood backer cut square and flush to the outside edges. Illustration **A** on page 118 shows simple box construction that is easily accomplished with a table saw or using just a router and a miter box. A number of corner joints such as dovetails and others obviously could be substituted as desired. The miter, step-by-step box glue-up procedure is described and illustrated in **B** to **F** on pages 118 and 119. *Tip:* Before applying any glue, make a dry run to check for joint tightness and a square assembly.

The intarsia lid may be attached with small hinges. Or, a rabbet, slightly wider than the wall thickness, can be cut all around the edges so the lid fits into the opening and is supported by the "lip."

Any square or rectangular intarsia design given in this book can be incorporated into a similar box utilizing the preceeding techniques.

The lighthouse intarsia piece completed.

Cape Lookout Lighthouse Box.

Cape Lookout Lighthouse Box

Full-size pattern for box lid.

Use $1/4$" x $5^3/4$" x $7^5/8$" material and $1/4$" plywood backer or size to suit.

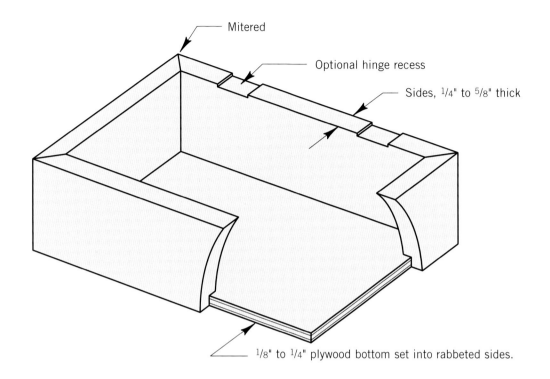

Mitered

Optional hinge recess

Sides, $^1/_4$" to $^5/_8$" thick

$^1/_8$" to $^1/_4$" plywood bottom set into rabbeted sides.

A. Simple square or rectangular box construction.

Lay the box sides inside facedown and end-to-end, as shown. Apply a piece of painter's blue masking tape tightly across each joint.

Flip the taped pieces over and apply glue to the mitered surfaces.

"Roll" the pieces together, with the tape acting as hinges.

Tape the last corner joint tightly together.

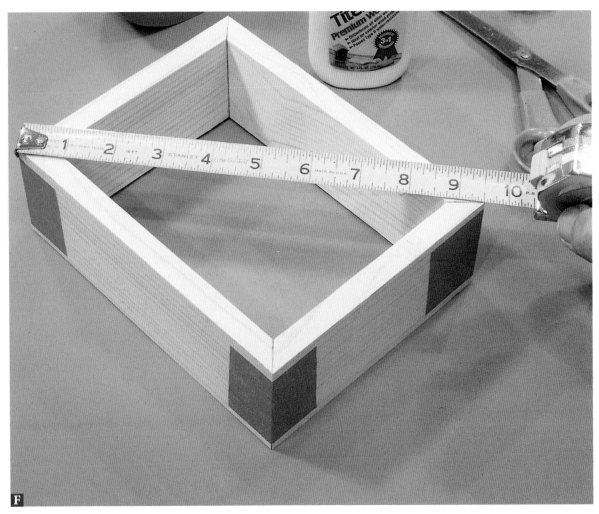

F

Check the diagonals for square and allow the glue to set.

Tumae Hopi Indian Doll Box

This colorful intarsia project can be enlarged for a wall decoration, worked into a paper towel holder, or used as a box lid as shown in **A** on *page 122*. The box-making techniques discussed here and in the folk-art flower box that follows can be used to make many similar boxes. Review the following designs that are workable for this style of box-making: Stars & Stripes *(page 34)*, Masai Shield *(page 35)*, Concrete Truck *(page 36)*, Dachshund Quilt *(page 46)*, Nutcracker Guard *(page 56)*, Happy and Sad Faces *(page 80)*, Dolphin *(page 82)*, Folk-Art Flowers Box *(page 124)*, and Stylized Fish *(page 90)*.

In addition to the intarsia piece, some thick wood is required (**B**, on *page 122*). If one solid piece is not available, laminate your own (**C**). Trace the edge profile from the intarsia piece onto the thick wood. Rabbet the edge of the intarsia piece (**D**) and lay out the appropriate wall thickness onto the thick wood, as shown in **E**.

Saw out the inside of the blank (**F** and **G**) to create the "sides" of the box. A bandsaw can also be used. Simply make an inward kerf cut with the grain that can be glued tight after sawing.

Glue a thin plywood bottom to the thick wood "ring" and bevel back the edges so they are not visible (**H**).

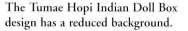

The Tumae Hopi Indian Doll Box design has a reduced background.

Full-size pattern or enlarge to suit.
Use $1/2$" or $5/8$" stock.
Reduce background to $3/8$" thickness.

Saw kerfs

**Tumae Hopi Indian
Doll Box**

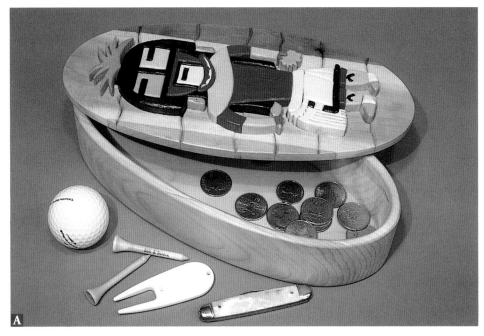

Unique boxes such as this with an intarsia lid are easy to make.

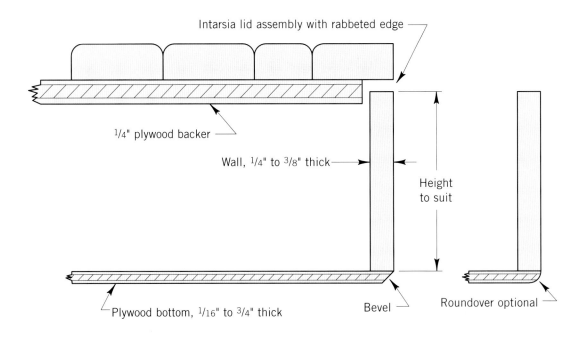

Intarsia lid assembly with rabbeted edge

1/4" plywood backer

Wall, 1/4" to 3/8" thick

Height to suit

Plywood bottom, 1/16" to 3/4" thick

Bevel

Roundover optional

B. Basic construction details for scroll-sawn or band-sawn boxes.

C Typical ¾-inch boards can be laminated face-to-face to create thick stock.

D The intarsia lid is rabbeted all around.

E The appropriate wall thickness is finger-gauged all around the sawn block.

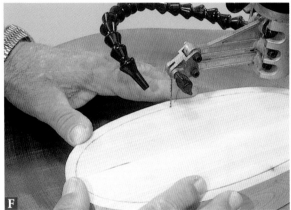

F Cutting out the box opening.

G The lid, box "ring," and the ¹/₁₆- or ⅛-inch plywood bottom.

H Sanding back the bottom edges so they are not visible.

Folk-Art Flowers Box

The simple oblong shape of the folk-art flower design and its simple intarsia detailing make it perfect for a box lid. The same techniques used to make the Tumae Hopi Indian Doll Box are employed to make this project (**A** and **B**).

This folk-art intarsia piece makes another good box top, and the same design is also incorporated into the Folk-Art Flowers Paper-Towel Holder illustrated on page 126.

This oblong folk-art flower design makes another nice box.

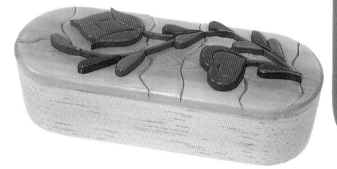

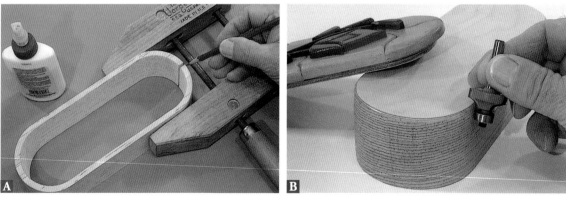

A This extra-thick stock was band-sawn. The inside entry kerf, sawn with the grain, will be glued shut.

B A round-over bit cuts back the ⅛-inch plywood edge so it is not visible. Also shown here is the relief of the intarsia lid and the rabbeted edge.

Full-size pattern or
enlarge to suit.
Use $3/4$" stock and
$1/8$" plywood backer.
Reduce background
to $1/2$" thickness.

Top edge,
$3/16$" radius.

**Folk-Art
Flowers Box**

Folk-Art Flowers Paper-Towel Holder

Here is another vertical design of a folk-art flower that makes an interesting wall plaque as is and as a slightly different presentation for a paper-towel holder (**A**, on *page 129*). In this project, the intarsia piece is set in from the rear. A rabbeted edge all around the scroll-sawn and routed opening provides a gluing surface. Refer to the section details given in the patterns on *page 128*.

This project also features an optional knob which threads onto the top of the large dowel, making the project more "user friendly" (see **B** and **C**, on *page 130*).

This intarsia design is made the same as that used for the Folk-Art Flowers Box on pages 124 and 125. See pages 127 and 128 for the patterns.

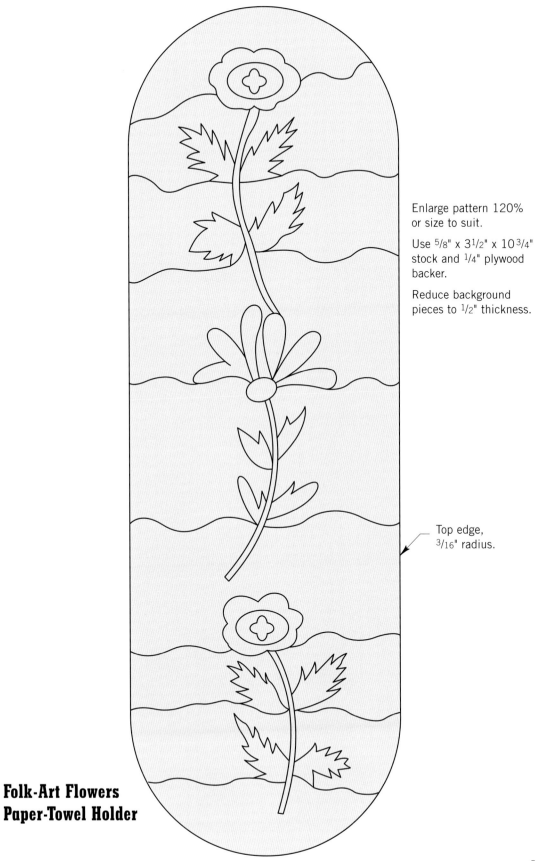

Enlarge pattern 120% or size to suit.

Use $5/8$" x $3 1/2$" x $10 3/4$" stock and $1/4$" plywood backer.

Reduce background pieces to $1/2$" thickness.

Top edge, $3/16$" radius.

Folk-Art Flowers Paper-Towel Holder

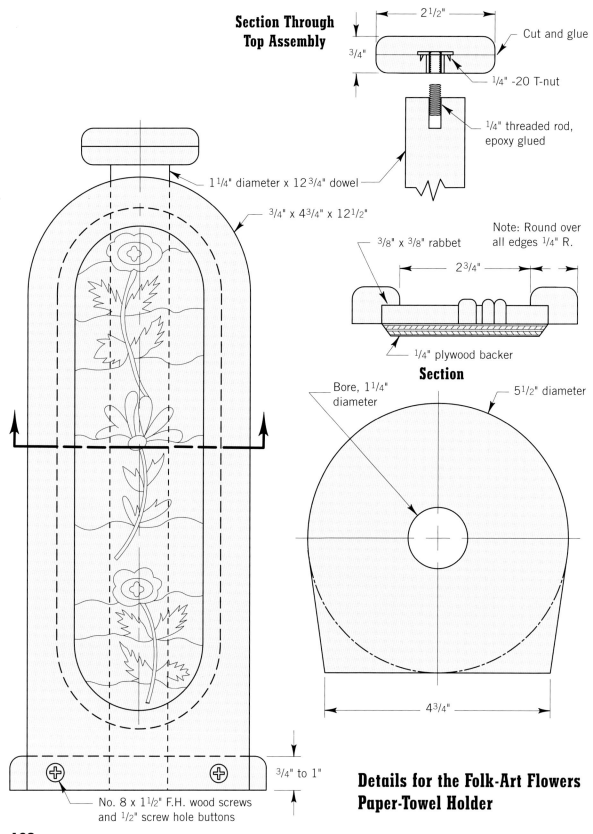

2 1/2"

3/4"

Cut and glue

1/4" -20 T-nut

1/4" threaded rod,
epoxy glued

1 1/4" diameter x 12 3/4" dowel

3/4" x 4 3/4" x 12 1/2"

Note: Round over
all edges 1/4" R.

3/8" x 3/8" rabbet

2 3/4"

1/4" plywood backer

Section

Bore, 1 1/4"
diameter

5 1/2" diameter

4 3/4"

3/4" to 1"

No. 8 x 1 1/2" F.H. wood screws
and 1/2" screw hole buttons

Details for the Folk-Art Flowers
Paper-Towel Holder

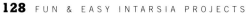

A. The intarsia for this paper-towel holder is set in from the rear, and glued to a rabbeted lid cut around a scroll-sawn opening.

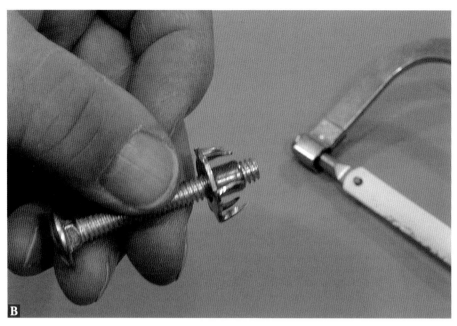

A cut-off length of a ¼-inch bolt and a T-nut are the key components for making the threaded knob shown in A.

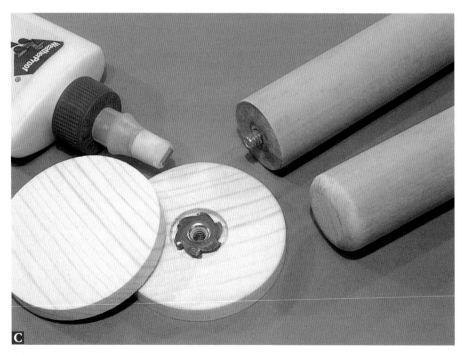

The T-nut is sandwiched between two round pieces glued together, and the threaded rod is epoxy-glued into the dowel end.

Uncle Sam Paper-Towel Holder

This intarsia piece begins with ¾-inch solid wood. Various pieces are cut thinner, and the hat-brim piece is tapered on its surface and shimmed ¼ inch. Additional shaping details are given in the pattern on the following page. Note that the bottom shoulder piece and the hat brim are the only pieces cut from horizontal grain.

The paper-towel holder shown on *page 133* is easily made with a simple base and a dowel. Review the previous paper-towel holder projects *(pages 126 to 130).*

The Uncle Sam intarsia makes a great patriotic decoration wherever it is displayed.

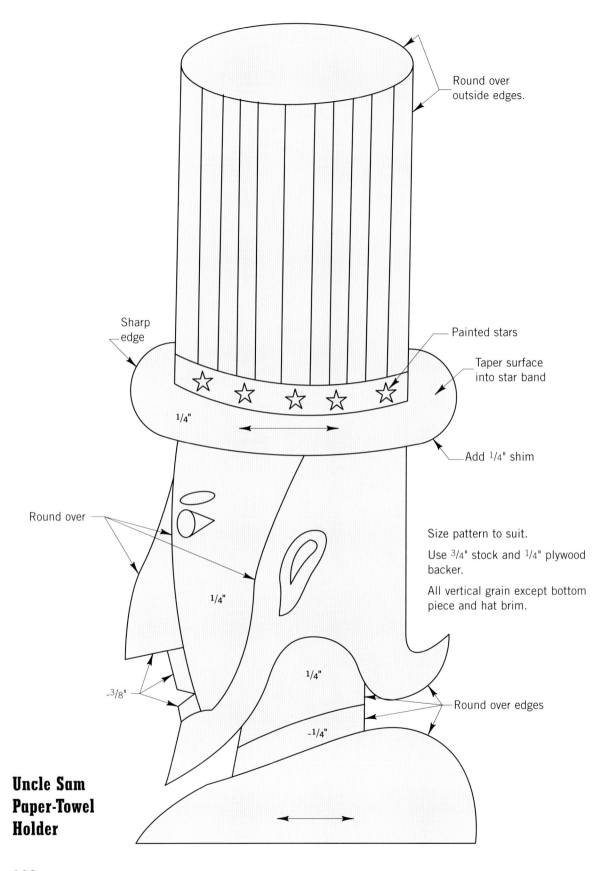

Round over
outside edges.

Sharp
edge

Painted stars

Taper surface
into star band

1/4"

Add 1/4" shim

Round over

1/4"

Size pattern to suit.

Use 3/4" stock and 1/4" plywood
backer.

All vertical grain except bottom
piece and hat brim.

-3/8"

1/4"

Round over edges

-1/4"

Uncle Sam
Paper-Towel
Holder

Uncle Sam Paper-Towel Holder.

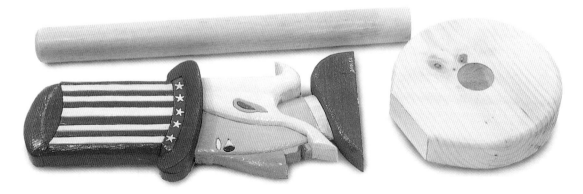

The components ready for assembly.

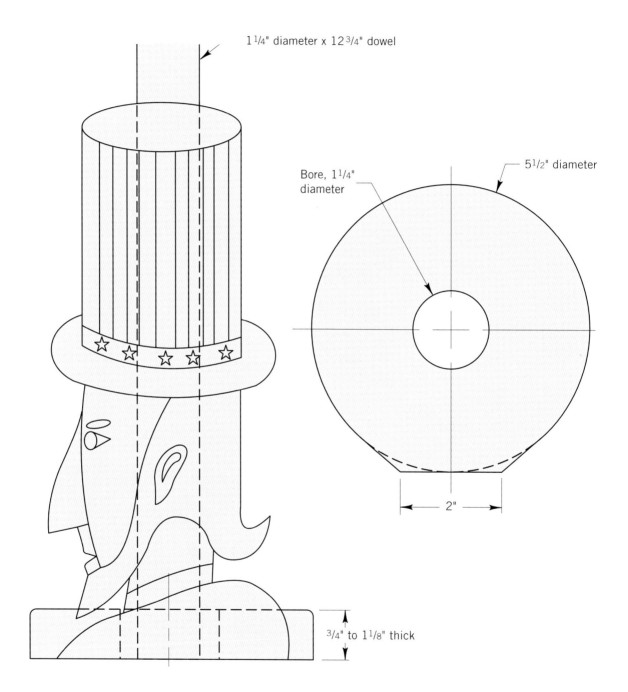

1 1/4" diameter x 12 3/4" dowel

Bore, 1 1/4" diameter

5 1/2" diameter

2"

3/4" to 1 1/8" thick

Patterns for the Uncle Sam Paper-Towel Holder.

Happy Frog Pegboard

A variety of the design patterns provided in this book can be utilized as decorative overlays on pegboard projects. The Happy Frog is a good example.

Simply trace the profile onto a wide board at a suitable location. Then develop the outside profile for the entire project using the pattern on *page 136* as a guide. The edge of the intarsia assembly is rabbeted all around, as shown in **F**, on *page 137*.

The objective is to make the premade intarsia piece appear as a relatively thin overlay. This is accomplished by fitting the backer side of it into a routed recess as shown in **A** to **F**, on *page 137*. A few alternative designs that could be worked into similar pegboards are: Stars & Stripes *(page 34)*, Turtle Party Guy *(page 37)*, Swordfish *(page 40)*, Happy and Sad Faces *(page 80)*, and Tropical Fish Mantle Clock, which follows.

Happy Frog Pegboard. See the pattern on page 136.

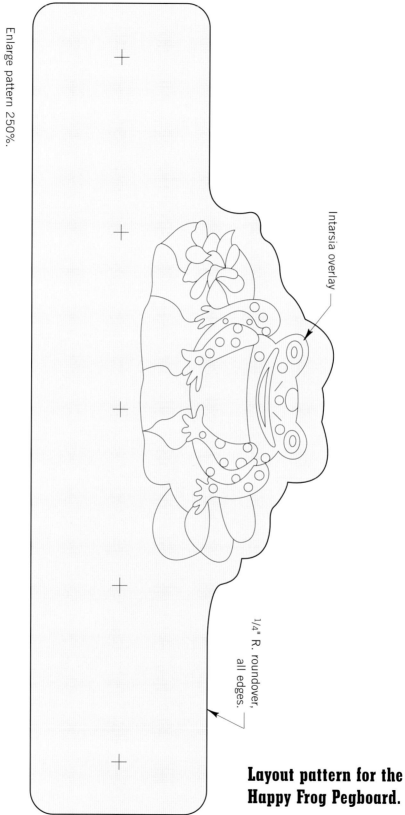

Enlarge pattern 250%.
Use 3/4" x 8¼" x 21¼" material.

Intarsia overlay

¼" R. roundover,
all edges.

**Layout pattern for the
Happy Frog Pegboard.**

A

The "washer trick" makes drawing a line parallel to the general profile shape easy.

B

Round over sharp, inside corners to create a profile edge that the pilot of a round-over bit can follow.

C

Making a "pencil rubbing" of the back to create a pattern for routing a recess.

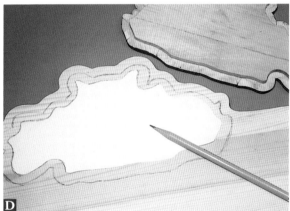

D

The "rubbing" pattern for routing a recess is scissor-cut to size and then traced, as shown.

E

Freehand-routing a rough-sized recess to receive the rabbeted intarsia piece.

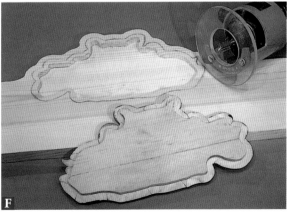

F

The completed router-cut recess ready for the rabbeted intarsia piece.

Tropical Fish Mantle Clock

The intarsia tropical-fish design is a low-relief project that may be incorporated into a number of useful projects, including this mantle clock (shown on *pages 140* and *141*). The arched frame is cut from 1¾- to 2-inch-thick stock, with the remaining inside piece resawn to a ¾-inch thickness, which then becomes the face panel (**A** to **C**, on *page 142*).

The intarsia inlay piece should be made from solid wood no thicker than ⅜ inch and use a ⅛-inch plywood backer. The inlay is made by bevel-sawing the intarsia piece while it is fastened to the front panel with double-face tape. Refer to bevel-sawing techniques in *The New Scroll Saw Handbook*. Be sure to make test cuts on scrap to ensure that the blade and bevel angle combination are correct.

The next steps are to make the glued assembly, make and attach the base, apply a finish, and install the clock insert (**F**, on *page 143*). Other designs or partial designs that may be substituted as inlays for this clock are: Turtle Party Guy *(page 37)* and Stylized Fish *(page 90)*.

This tropical fish is a low-relief design that is best made from thin materials when used as an inlay.

Close-up that shows small cut-outs of the eye pieces and the rotary tool texturing.

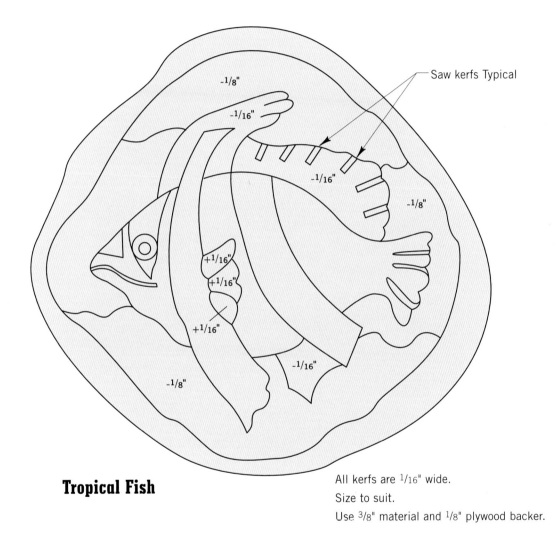

Saw kerfs Typical

-1/8"

-1/16"

-1/16"

-1/8"

+1/16"

+1/16"

+1/16"

-1/8"

-1/16"

Tropical Fish

All kerfs are 1/16" wide.
Size to suit.
Use 3/8" material and 1/8" plywood backer.

This mantle clock project requires
careful sawing of thick wood.

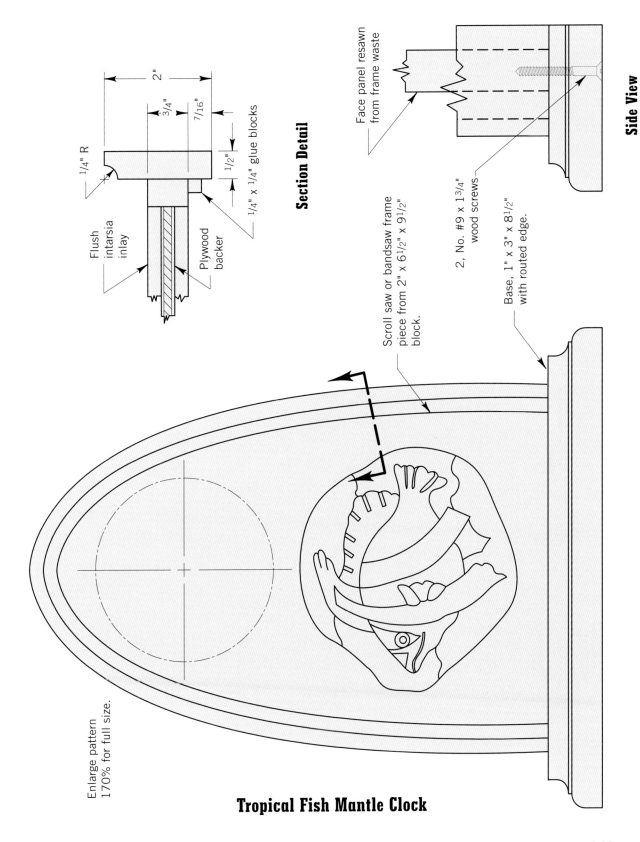

Section Detail

2"

3/4" 7/16"

1/4" R

1/2"

1/4" x 1/4" glue blocks

Flush intarsia inlay

Plywood backer

Side View

Face panel resawn from frame waste

2, No. #9 x 1³/₄" wood screws

Base, 1" x 3" x 8¹/₂" with routed edge.

Scroll saw or bandsaw frame piece from 2" x 6¹/₂" x 9¹/₂" block.

Enlarge pattern 170% for full size.

Tropical Fish Mantle Clock

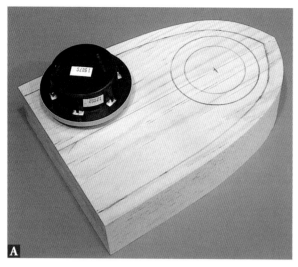

A Two-inch-thick stock laid out for inside sawing.

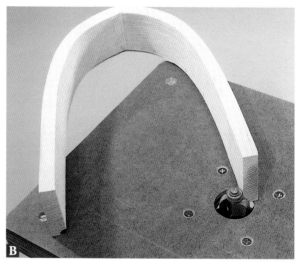

B Routing the inside edge of the arched frame piece.

C The completed components. Note the face panel, which is the inside piece remaining from sawing the thick arch. It was then subsequently resawn to a ¾-inch thickness.

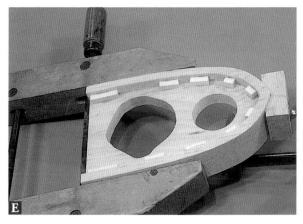

D

Clamping the face panel to the arched frame.

E

This rear view shows the use of glue blocks.

F

A close-up that shows the nice fit of the small intarsia inlay.

Lighthouse Bulletin Board

The lighthouse overlay shown in this project is one more example of ways to use designs from this book. The frame involves basic construction techniques. Obviously, other frame styles are usable. Frames can be made to any size desired and also hung vertically if desired. Another idea is to substitute acrylic mirror, which can be cut easily with woodworking tools. A silicon adhesive is recommended for gluing wood pieces to acrylic.

Some other intarsia designs that might be used as mirror or bulletin-board projects are: Swordfish *(page 40),* Native-American Design *(page 60),* Fast Car *(page 76),* Dolphin *(page 82),* Stylized Fish *(page 90),* Tumae Hopi Indian Doll Box *(page 120),* Uncle Sam Paper-Towel Holder *(page 131),* and Dragon Wall Cabinet *(page 154).*

One-eighth-inch-thick sheet cork is available from arts and crafts mail-order companies in rolls 48 inches wide or in smaller sheets up to 24 x 36 inches. Simply glue it to a sheet of ¼-inch plywood using yellow glue or contact cement. Illustrations **A** to **I**, on *pages 146* and *147,* provide helpful information.

A cork-faced bulletin board with a glued-on intarsia lighthouse design from Memories (page 98).

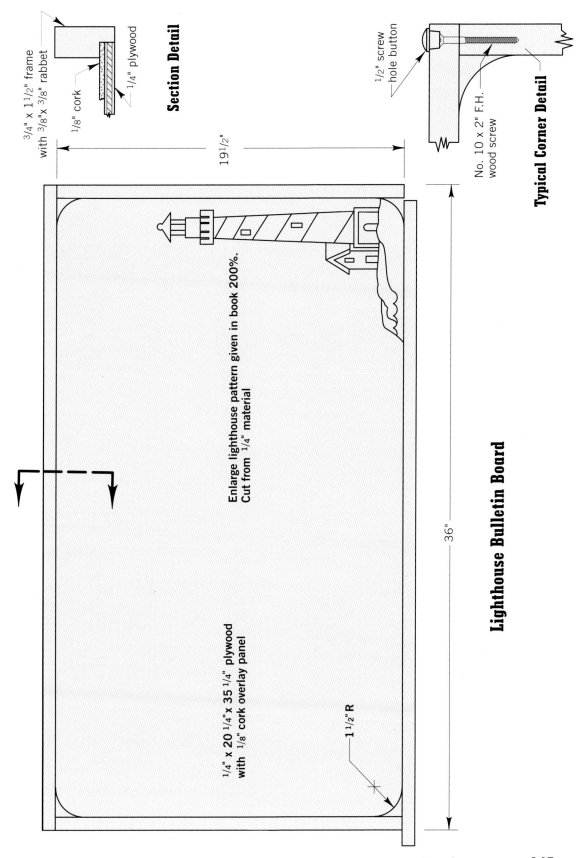

Section Detail

3/4" x 1 1/2" frame
with 3/8" x 3/8" rabbet

1/8" cork

1/4" plywood

19 1/2"

Typical Corner Detail

1/2" screw
hole button

No. 10 x 2" F.H.
wood screw

36"

Enlarge lighthouse pattern given in book 200%.
Cut from 1/4" material

1/4" x 20 1/4" x 35 1/4" plywood
with 1/8" cork overlay panel

1 1/2" R

Lighthouse Bulletin Board

A

Inside corner blocks glued in place.

B

Smoothing out the corners.

C

Rabbeting the rear of the frame. A strip of wood clamped to the frame provides more surface support for the router.

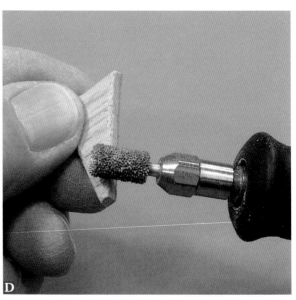

D

Rounding the edges of the lighthouse segments with a rotary tool.

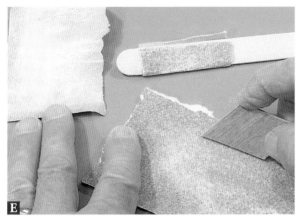

E

Rounding over by hand.

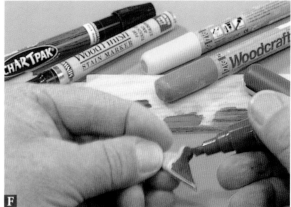

F

Coloring small parts with felt markers.

G

Using wood stain markers.

H

The finished pieces ready to be glued down.

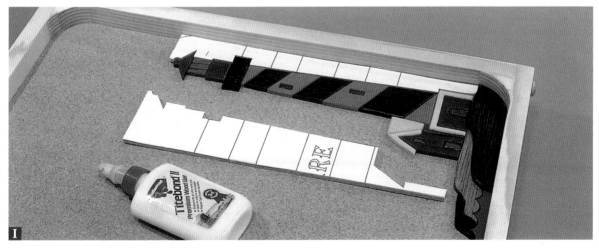

I

Using the waste pieces (shown with the paper pattern still attached) to help align and position the individual pieces for gluing.

Hanging Flowers Inlay Table

This project is an excellent example of how easily a piece of intarsia can be inlaid into a table top. The "leg and stub rail" design shown here is used for three-leg round or triangular tables, but oblong, oval, square, or rectangular tables with four legs can be made almost as easily. These alternative intarsia designs from projects may be substituted for round tables: Native-American Design *(page 60)*, Old-Time Sailing Ship *(page 72)*, Pennsylvania Dutch Hex Design Inlaid Plate *(page 114)*. Previous square and rectangular designs are too numerous to list.

Review the fundamental construction details given on *page 151*. *Tip:* Consider making four legs even when making the three-leg table. Legs are removable, so should you ever want to make another, different-shaped table, you will have the extra leg.

The table is designed so the top is "free floating."

That is, it is not fastened to any part of the table. It is supported by a piece of ¼-inch plywood to which the legs are attached with screws. A protective piece of "free-floating" ⅛-inch clear acrylic lies over the top.

The intarsia inlay piece can be inlaid in several ways:

1. It can be made to slip into an opening sawn completely through the top (**B** to **D**, on *page 152*).

2. It can be made to fit into a compass or freehand routed recess cut partially into the surface. In this case, the top could be made reversible with another design on the opposite side if desired.

3. The inlay could also be inserted from the bottom as done with the Folk-Art Flowers Paper-Towel Holder *(page 126)*.

The remaining major steps are illustrated and described in **E** to **I**, on p*age 153*.

Hanging flowers intarsia.

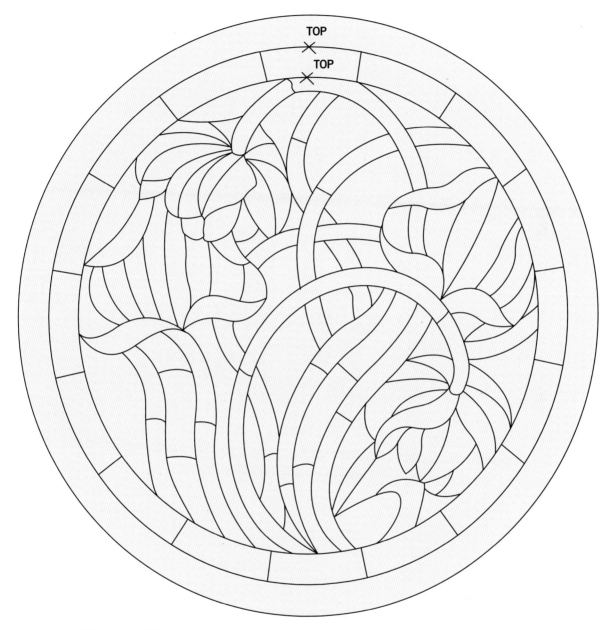

Hanging Flowers
(Stained-glass style)

Enlarge pattern 125% or size to suit.
Use 1/4" material and 1/4" plywood backer.

A chair-shaped side table with round intarsia and a hanging flowers inlay.

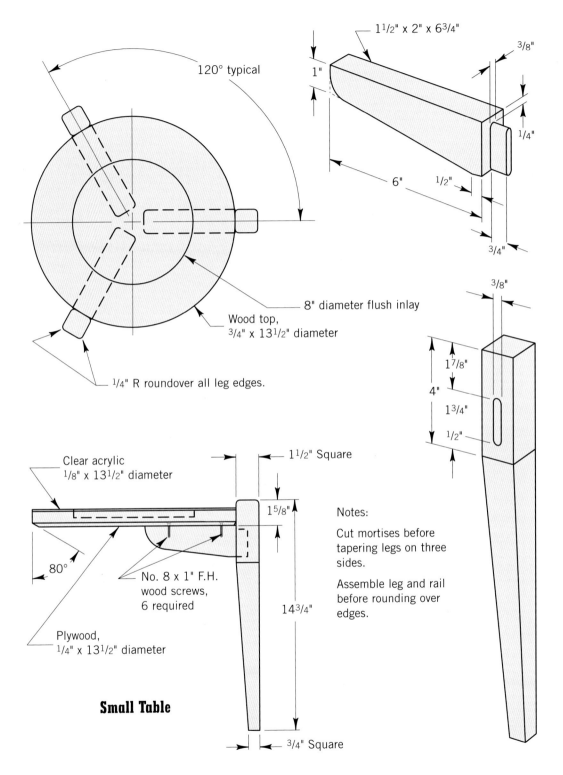

120° typical

1 1/2" x 2" x 6 3/4"

3/8"

1"

1/4"

6"   1/2"

3/4"

8" diameter flush inlay

Wood top,
3/4" x 13 1/2" diameter

1/4" R roundover all leg edges.

3/8"

1 7/8"

4"

1 3/4"

1/2"

Clear acrylic
1/8" x 13 1/2" diameter

1 1/2" Square

1 5/8"

80°

No. 8 x 1" F.H.
wood screws,
6 required

Plywood,
1/4" x 13 1/2" diameter

14 3/4"

3/4" Square

Small Table

Notes:

Cut mortises before
tapering legs on three
sides.

Assemble leg and rail
before rounding over
edges.

Construction details for chair-shaped side table.

 A

View showing the inlay in a round tabletop.

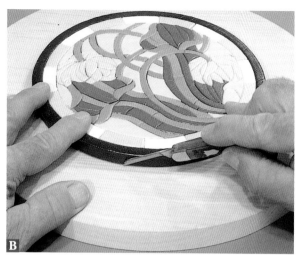

B

A knife point scribes a sharp cutting line around the intarsia piece.

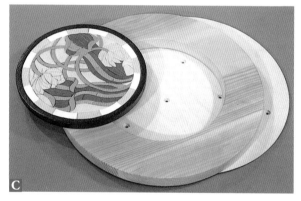

C

From left to right: intarsia inlay top; scroll-sawn, cut-through opening; and a ¼-inch plywood support.

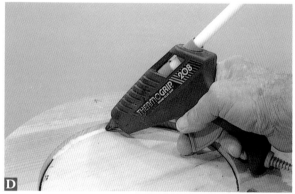

D

A bead of hot-melt adhesive applied to the bottom, as shown, keeps the inlay flush on the top surface.

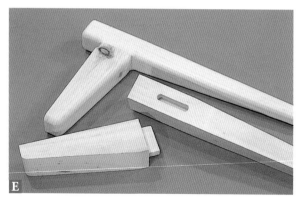

E

Simple leg-and-stub rail construction involves mortise-and-tenon joinery, tapering, and rounding over.

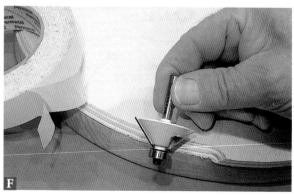

F

The ¼-inch plywood supporting the free-floating top is simultaneously sized and beveled using the top as a routing pattern.

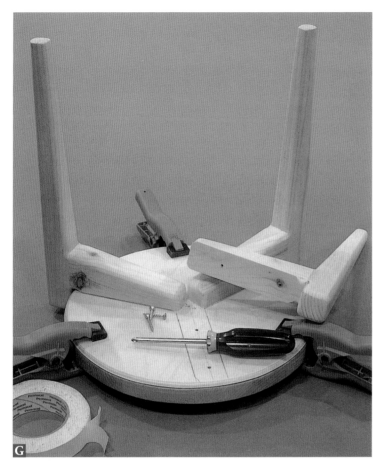

The assembly is held snugly together and each leg rail location is marked.

The plywood support is screwed to the legs (from the top down). The tabletop itself is not attached at all. It is kept in place by the "bumper effect" of the legs.

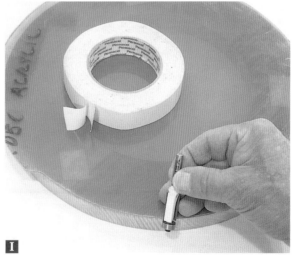

A piece of ⅛-inch-thick acrylic (shown with a protective film) is routed to size using the floating top as a pattern and a flush trim bit.

Dragon Wall Cabinet

A wide variety of chest-panel and cabinet-door projects can incorporate a piece of intarsia to add visual interest and value. The dragon intarsia design has many uses in the hands of a creative woodworker.

There are also a number of the previous designs that may be incorporated into cabinet doors and/or panels. To name just a few, they are: Masai Shield *(page 35),* Maple Leaf Quilt *(page 52),* and Nutcracker Guard *(page 56).* Of course, almost any rectangular design can be used as well.

The small wall cabinet illustrated below is easily modified to a larger size than as detailed on *pages 156* and *157.* Make the intarsia plaque overlay with a rabbeted edge so it sets into a scroll-sawn opening cut through the door. Alternatively, it can be set into a routed recess cut to the appropriate depth. Review the Folk-Art Flowers Paper-Towel Holder *(page 126),* which illustrates other overlay or inlay-mounting techniques that can be adapted to this project.

The dragon is a multilevel intarsia piece.

Dragon intarsia as a wall clock.

Taper toward tongue

-1/8"

-1/8"   -1/8"

-1/8"

-1/8"   -1/8"   -1/8"

-1/8"

Enlarge pattern
115% or size
to suit.

Use 5/8" or
3/4" stock,
6" x 10 1/4".

Reduce back-
ground to 7/16"
thickness.

Shape crest
and tail pieces
before cutting
into segments.

Reduce tail 1/8"
in thickness.

Dragon

The dragon wall cabinet is a small, easy-to-make project.

This rear view shows the rabbet cut to receive the plywood back and the glue blocks at the inside corner of the sides and the front rail.

A thin piece of plywood, tacked inside the door as shown, hides the backer side of the rabbeted overlay of the dragon intarsia assembly.